Married 4 Life

BUILD A MARRIAGE THAT LASTS A LIFETIME

BY

SCOT AND HOLLY ANDERSON

18 17 16 15 10 9 8 7 6 5 4 3 2 1

Married 4 Life: Build a Marriage That Lasts a Lifetime
ISBN 13: 978-168031-014-6
Copyright © 2015 by Scot Anderson
Mesa, AZ 85213

Published by Harrison House Publishers
Tulsa, OK 74145
www.harrisonhouse.com

Contents

CHAPTER
1

THE LAST FIGHT YOU
WILL EVER HAVE

Nearly every marriage that ends in divorce happens because of one last fight. Usually it is an accumulation of many fights, but it is that one last fight that takes the marriage over the edge and ends it once and for all. Nearly all marital frustration comes from arguments and fights. Think about your own marriage. What would you love to do without? If a genie granted you one marital wish what would it be? Better sex? (Okay, that affects a few minutes a day.) That your spouse treated you better? That you got more out of the marriage? To be happier in your marriage? What would be your wish?

Well, if you wished for your fights to be milder and only last a few minutes, you would get all of the above. What if you could take away all the stupid fights and fights over nothing, and then take the leftover fights and get out of them in less than five minutes? And when I say "out," I mean out! Not one spouse pouting, not one spouse saying, "Hey, let's ignore this fight but stay mad at each other." I'm saying, "You are out of the fight—the past is the past, and we enjoy the moment!"

If you did this, how much happier would you be? How much more time would you have to enjoy your spouse, and life for that matter? Think about how much time you waste on stupid fights, being mad and upset. How many late nights did you stay up arguing the same point over and over? How many hurtful things did you waste time saying? How many hurtful things said to you wasted your mental energy—replaying over and over in your mind?

Holly and I have been happily married for nineteen years. Now, we have been married for twenty-two years, but the key word is *happily*. Those first three years were hell—fight after fight, argument after argument. We fought over every stupid thing you could imagine. Our battles lasted days, weeks, even months. Those fights were like athletes foot—just when you thought you beat them, they were back again, annoying the heck out of you!

One day while having lunch with my mom, I got the idea for five minute fights. At this point in my life, I had been married and out of the house for nearly three years. To give you a little background, I grew up in a very loving home with the best parents, yet they fought constantly. My parents knew how to argue; they were masters at it. I would say they were the Samurai Warriors of fighting! They were definitely well-skilled in the art. Their fights lasted for what seemed like days at a time. Most of my parents' fights seemed dumb to me even as a child. I remember thinking things like: *Get over it. Why are you so mad? Didn't you have this fight last week? Just let it go, it's not that big of a deal.* It's funny how that childlike wisdom seemed to slip when I got married, and I found myself repeating these same fights with my wife that I used to think were dumb and immature.

As my mom and I were enjoying our lunch, her phone rang. I could tell it was my dad on the other end, so I just sat back and watched as a fight ensued. It happened so quickly! It brought me back to my childhood years. I took a bite of my sandwich as I watched my fight mentors go at it. It actually felt good to watch someone else fight for a change. However, less than a minute into the battle, my mom said "WHATEVER!" then hung up the phone. I tried to hold back my smile as I asked, "So trouble in paradise?"

My mom shook her head slightly, and then with a dazed expression said, "No, your father is just being a little annoying."

I smiled and said, "A little? Looked like he was a lot annoying."

Mom smiled and said, "Oh, your father is never a lot annoying. He's an amazing man." This shocked me! Not because he wasn't amazing; he surely was amazing. But in the midst of a battle, she was talking good about him. She then looked down for a moment and mumbled, "I better call him. It bothers him if he thinks I'm upset."

I looked around to see if I was on some kind of hidden camera show, or maybe Jesus was coming back. I just witnessed something I had never seen before! I just saw a unicorn. In the middle of an argument, who thinks about the other person? Who gives a rip if they are upset? This makes no sense. Maybe Santa is for real?

As my mom reached for her phone, it rang. She picked it up and said, "I'm sorry."

You could tell my dad said, "No, I'm sorry."

"No, it was my fault." (Once again, I could tell that Dad tried to take the blame.) "Alright, I love you, see you in a bit." Then my mom hung up the phone, looked up at me and smiled. I honestly would have been less surprised if she spouted wings and flew a couple laps around the food court.

"What just happened," I stuttered.

"What," my mom responded as she took a small bite of her salad.

"That's not how my parents fight. How in the world did you stop fighting so fast?"

"Oh, we haven't fought in years," my mom responded. "And when we do, it never lasts more than a few minutes."

I hadn't been around my parents much the past seven or eight years because I was in college, dating, and then of course, spending a lot of time with Holly. So since I was not living at home, it never occurred to me that their fighting had ended. I left that lunch on a quest. I would discover this unicorn of philosophies, this fairytale of folklore—that you could actually be in a relationship in which you didn't argue or fight, and when you did fight, it would only last a few minutes.

I went home and told Holly this exciting news, and we fought about it and a lot of other stuff! Then we got my parents' marriage seminars and marriage books. We also bought other books and went to marriage seminars of our own. It wasn't long before we were doing all that you will read in this book. We were living the same dream that took my parents thirty years to discover. We were living year three of our marriage. Holly and I want you to enjoy this amazing dream in your marriage too, so we wrote this book to help you. Here is what you will learn in this book:

1. The source of all arguments.

2. The needs of a man (and no, they are not just sleep, food, and sex) and the needs of a woman (and no, they are not so complicated that even God doesn't know what they are). Most arguments stem from our needs not being met. They aren't being met because our spouse doesn't know what our needs are. And in most cases, we don't even know what they are ourselves. Holly and I were amazed at how many dumb fights came out of these needs that we didn't even know existed.

3. How each of our needs compliment the needs of the other. Ultimately, we need each other.

4. How easy it is to live a life meeting the needs of our spouse, and that in meeting these needs, we stir up the fire of passion in our marriage.

5. How meeting our spouse's needs helps meet our own needs.

6. That sometimes our relationship *needs* an argument. Learn how to argue in a constructive way. A constructive argument sharpens us and helps us to become better by establishing rules and boundaries in the relationship. But it is important to know how to argue.

7. How to get in and out of an argument in five minutes and eliminate most of the dumb fights.

8. How to forgive.

9. How to control emotions, before, during, and after a fight.

10. How *not* to fight, even when your spouse really wants to.

Through these ten things, we will show you how to bring passion back into your marriage. You will learn what love really is and how to fall in love with your spouse all over again. You will experience true intimacy! In the end, you will learn how to experience a fairytale marriage that lives *happily ever after*.

YOUR GREATEST BATTLE WILL ALWAYS BE U!

The Tooth Fairy Doesn't Have Verizon

In my house, the tooth fairy has been a very irresponsible person. Let me be honest with you, we have one of the worst tooth fairies the world has ever known. My wife has on many occasions referred to the tooth fairy as lazy, inconsiderate, self-centered, and unusually cheap. Our tooth fairy would sometimes go months before he would grab the tooth and leave some money. By then, of course, the tooth is literally going back to dirt.

One day I decided that I was going to be the greatest tooth fairy ever. Our children were going to sing songs about this tooth fairy, and tell great tales of his exploits. So when Savvy, our daughter, was five years old and lost her first tooth, the tooth fairy was on it. BOOM! I was there the first night and snatched that thing up. I threw ten bucks under her pillow. BOOM! I nailed that thing!

I asked my wife, "Who is the greatest tooth fairy ever?" She did not respond. The next morning, Savvy came out screaming "Yeaaaah!" while waving her $10 bill. Of course, all of her brothers were envious and said things like, "Oh my gosh, our tooth fairy never shows up! I still have a tooth from when I was eight. I never got more than a dollar!"

I was feeling pretty confident after nailing that first tooth but a week later, tooth number two came out. When that night came and the tooth fairy checked under the pillow, he discovered that Holly and Savvy had obviously forgotten to put the tooth under the pillow. No big deal, right? So tooth fairy checked the second night, but still no tooth. Now, we discovered that a man's simple mind (or the tooth fairy's simple mind) has an attention span of two days, because the tooth fairy forgot all about the tooth from that point forward.

Fast forward to Sunday a week later. I'm in the bathroom getting ready for church. Outside of the door, I heard Savvy crying and Holly consoling her. Savvy said the tooth fairy hadn't shown up for a couple nights. Springing into action (the man's mind is *so* quick), I grabbed hold of the solution right off the bat. I waited just a few moments and then I opened the door with my phone up to my ear. I put it down and said, "Savvy, I just got off the phone with the tooth fairy and the tooth fairy said sorry about last night. Things got busy, but she'll be there tonight with a special treat."

That was AMAZING! I thought Holly would be like, "Oh my God, I love you so much, let's make love later." I literally thought I was like a savior riding in on the white steed. But instead, the love of my life looked at me, shook her head and said, "Sweetie, the tooth fairy doesn't have a phone." There was a long, awkward pause, so I want us all to pause as well to think about this statement: The tooth fairy doesn't have a cell phone. In essence, my wife was basically calling me either a fool or a liar in front of our daughter. I stood there like a deer in head lights, just staring, while my mind tried to process this. Then I said, "Honey" in the sweetest, kindest voice I could muster. I tried to stay calm. I knew there was a fight coming, but I wanted to set it up for this five minute in-and-out thing. I said, "Now, I just want to make sure we're talking about the same magical tooth fairy here. Are we discussing the magical tooth fairy that goes into millions of homes in just one night? How could that be possible? This same magical tooth fairy breaks in without anyone knowing and puts money under the kid's pillow? And *magically* has money for every child—millions of dollars, although the tooth fairy doesn't have a job or any stable income? This is the magical tooth fairy that you are discussing in front of Savanna? Now you are saying that I have somehow stretched the truth far beyond imagination by saying that the tooth fairy stopped at the Verizon store over the weekend and got a cell phone? I'm the liar?"

This book will be of no use to you unless you get this one point. There is only one person in the world you have the power to change—YOU! You can't change your spouse, your friend, or your boss. *You only have the power to change you.* The biggest problem in marriages today is that you have two people who are each trying to change the other person. It's like trying to make a stranger's car go where *you* want it to go. Try it. Today while driving down the road, try and make some stranger's car go to your house. You will have to swerve at them, cut them off, and try and force them to turn. Chances are you will crash and the cops will arrest you. It is impossible to make their car do what you want it to do! *But you can control your own car.* You can easily drive it right to the destination you want. It's the same way in life. Many people spend their days trying to get other cars to go where they want to go, rather than just driving their car of life to where they want to go.

This book is not for your spouse. It was not intended for you to highlight all the parts your spouse needs to read. This book was intended for *you*. This book will not work if you spend your time saying, "He sure needs this," or "This will really help her." No! This book is for you to work on yourself and change yourself. This book is to help you become the best you possible. What happens if we get two people in a marriage, both trying to be the best they can be? We get an amazing marriage. What do we get when we have two people trying to make the other person the best they can be? We get a horrible marriage. What I want you to realize is that if you change *you*, you will bring change to your spouse.

Let me give you an example. Let's say you have been trying to change your wife for years, but she never changes. She is a mean ol' female dog. But what if you became an amazing husband? What if you got up a little earlier every morning and did something special for her? For my wife, this means driving to Starbucks. What if you then helped with the kids before you headed off to work, while keeping a good attitude? What if you texted your wife a few times during the day telling her how awesome she is? What if you dropped everything to talk to her when she calls? What if you came home and spent the first twenty minutes of the night sharing your day with her, and then letting her share hers? What if you helped her with dinner and the kids? If you did one or more of these things, we both know that you would see a noticeable difference in her. You basically changed her by changing you.

You may think, *Hey, that's sounds like a lot of work.* It's not a *lot*, but it is work. A great marriage takes work, time and effort. But anything of any worth always takes work. Being a great hunter takes a lot of work. Scouting out the area, setting up camp, getting your equipment ready, and giving the hunt your undivided attention. Talk about work. This is work! A great marriage that brings you and your children joy your entire lives, also takes hard work. But the rewards are priceless!

I love this quote: "Almost no one is foolish enough to believe he/she automatically deserves great success in any field of activity, yet almost everyone believes that he/she automatically deserves success in marriage." If you want to be a great piano player, you have to what? *Learn and practice.* If you want to be a great golfer, you have to learn and practice. If you want a great marriage, you have to learn and practice.

You will spend time one way or the other. You will spend time making a great marriage or you will spend time fighting and arguing within your horrible marriage. You will spend a lot of time if you choose divorce. Between courts, attorneys, driving kids back and forth, and the new relationship (which you will find needs the same work your old one needed), you discover that you have less time than you had before! Spend time to make your marriage great. Learn and then practice.

STOP FIGHTING YOURSELF, THE SOURCE OF ALL FIGHTS

The Hallmark Battle

The first five years of my marriage to Holly was a turbulent time. Tornado Scot-and-Holly touched down nearly every day! One day in particular, we were in a great battle over something so big and so important, that it had to be fought. I believe Holly said that I had said that I got off at 10, but I got home at 9 (which I would have thought was a good thing). I said, "No, I told you I got off at 9." This is was the classic *I said/no-you-didn't-you-lying-idiot* fight.

The fight began and I jabbed with some well-crafted comments about her spending, while she landed a few "you're a slob" accusations. I dodged and hit with a "*what do you do all day*" blow. The she countered with, "You work for your daddy." (Yes, a low blow). That hurt so I threw a huge right hand, landing the knockout punch with, "How often do we have sex?" This made her so mad, she had nothing to say. She ran to one of her drawers in the kitchen and pulled out a huge stack of Hallmark cards and began to rip them up and throw them in the air as she exclaimed, "These were on sale and I was saving you money, now look at me waste money!" She must have had a hundred plus cards that she ripped up, making it snow in our kitchen. This seemed so funny to me that I started to laugh. She stopped and cried out, "WHAT? What is so funny?" She then paused, looked around, and then we both began to laugh so hard we fell to the floor. Now every year on my birthday, I get a card that has been taped together. Now that is funny!

What if we said the source of all your fights could be found in you?

"Scot, are you saying all the fights are my fault?"

No, I'm not saying that. But I am saying that there is something in each of us that when triggered, leads us into an argument. In a sense, there is a button residing in you that when pushed, causes you to lose control and come out ready to fight. If we can get you to recognize this button and deal with the issues in you, this button will become very difficult to push, therefore eliminating most fights.

It takes two people to fight, so if you didn't engage in the fight, there would be no fight. You know the boxing game, Rock'em Sock'em Robots? As an older brother, I loved to annoy my younger brother. While playing Rock'em Sock'em, I would simply pull my guy back and sit there while Jason would bang and pound on his controls, his man swinging like a mad man at my guy. But his punches always fell just a little short because if my guy was pulled all the way back, there could be no contact. It wasn't long before Jason would get mad and leave. In a sense, this is what I'm talking about. If you don't swing, there is no fight. If you learn not to engage, the other person can swing all they want but there will be no fight. The goal isn't to be annoying of course; the goal is for you to be calm and have your head about you so you can steer the relationship out of the fight.

Most marriages are just like a Rock'em Sock'em fight—two crazy people throwing emotional blow after blow, trying to get the other person to lose their head. Finally, one person loses it and runs out crying, screaming, or throwing stuff. If we can show you why you lose your mind or say mean and hurtful things, this will help you control the urge to fight most of the time. In fact, this will eliminate literally eighty percent of your fights. Sometimes I lose it and Holly is cool and calm, while other times Holly loses it and I'm cool and calm. But it's awesome when Holly and I are both are cool and calm and there isn't a fight at all.

One force controls your "fight button." If you can master this force, you can maintain control. What is this powerful force that first took root in the garden with Adam and Eve? FEAR.

Second Timothy 1:7 tells us that God did not give us a spirit of fear, but control, love and a sound mind. God did not give you fear. He gave you *control*. What happens when that fear button in you gets pushed? You lose control. You lose control of your emotions and your actions. You also lose control of what you say and what you do. In the midst of a fight, you become someone else. You do things you would normally never do. You say things you never thought you would say. You say things to the love of your life that you wouldn't say to an enemy.

If we don't allow that fear button to be pushed, we remain in control. We command how we respond, how we act, what we say, and what we do. In a sense, we become the rudder of the "*Relation Ship*" by steering it out of trouble.

God did not give you fear. He gave you control and *love*. When that fear button gets pushed, you lose your ability to love. Everything you do in the midst of the fight lacks the element of love. It's interesting that the Bible says that love and fear cannot be in the same place. (1 John 4:18) When that fear button is pushed, you choose fear instead of love. But if you don't allow that fear button to be pushed, you can love your spouse right out of the argument. And once again, you become the rudder of the "*Relation Ship.*"

God did not give you fear but control, love and a *sound mind*. Let's be honest, in the midst of a fight, both spouses sound and act like a couple of eight year-olds. Think about Holly ripping those cards up? Now, that was funny, and a little crazy! Honestly, I act like a maniac when that fear button gets pushed in me. (I once threw a piece of molding across the garage and it pierced the wall and stuck out both sides.) If we don't allow that fear button to be pushed, we can, with a sound mind, be the rudder of the *Relation Ship*.

Let me show you how fear is responsible for your arguments. First, let me say that fear is the root of every negative emotion.

- *Stress and Worry* = Fear that things won't work out the way you want them to.

- *Depression* = Fear that things will never get better.

- *Anger* = Fear that you lost control.

- *Bitterness* = Fear that whoever hurt you won't be

punished.

- *Negative Attitude* = Fear that fate is against you.
- Think of your own negative emotions. One way or the other, they always come back to fear.
- In the same way, all positive emotions come from faith.
- *Peace* = Faith that things are working out.
- *Calm* = Faith that you are in control.
- *Joy* = Faith that things are good.
- *Positive Attitude* = Faith that things are going to get better.

God wants our world to be formed by our faith, while Satan wants our world to be formed by our fear. Both approaches always work. Faith will bring into your world what you are believing for, just as fear will bring about what you are most afraid of. And once you get what you are afraid of, you will then be reminded of how your fear was justified.

Take for example a guy who is very jealous. Jealousy is a fear of loss. Many jealous men were once very normal but out of fear, they lost control, lost the ability to love, and most definitely lost their sound mind. They end up hiding in the bushes, sneaking around, following their wives, hacking their email, checking their texts, and tracking their cars. They worry about the way their wives dress up for work. Are they wearing perfume? Earrings? Before long, their wives feel trapped and suffocated and can't live under that sort of control. They finally leave and this confirms their husbands' fear of loss, reminding them that the next time they need to be even more controlling.

Fear brings to you what you are afraid of. Fear shows you and then reminds you why you should be afraid. Fear is a relationship killer. Until you identify your fear button, it will continue to control you. Let me give you some fear examples.

- *Fear of being controlled.* If you ask someone who is afraid of being controlled to do something, they will rise up against you. No one controls *them*. For this person, a lot of fights come out of everyday circumstances where there should be no fight. The spouse simply asked them to clean up, act differently, or drive differently. Any time any amount of control is applied, they fight back. If this is you, then you need to deal with this fear.

- *Fear of losing control.* This person is a control freak and has to have everything their way, or they freak out. They get very mad, very fast. And there are so many opportunities to be angry, since the world tends to resist being controlled!

- *Fear of being wrong.* This person must always be right. They can never be wrong. Deep down they feel like if they are wrong, then something is wrong with them.

- *Fear of failure.* This person never tries anything. If they don't try, they'll never fail. They will run away instead—run away from hard times, run away from a marriage, and in doing so, they feel in some weird way as if they didn't fail because they never really tried.

- *Fear of not being accepted.* This person has a "Cain complex." The world must accept them as-is. They are unwilling to change. "If you truly accept me, then you accept the unacceptable." They use phrases like, "Well, this is just who I am." This person is bound by all their problems, never able to become a better person.

- *Fear of not being loved; fear of abandonment.* This fear can go one of two ways. The spouse may have to constantly prove their love. This person is very possessive, very smothering. They don't allow the other person to have any other life. Everything has to be about them. Or, conversely this person does everything for the other person. Not because they love them, but because they are afraid of losing their love. This is very unhealthy because you create a spoiled rotten spouse who is just a taker. Your fear of not being loved is actually coming true—you're not loved. You are simply being taken advantage of.

- *Fear of being worthless.* This person looks for reasons to feel worthless, so any criticism or critique drives them off the deep end. You can never do enough to please this person. What they want is for their spouse to give them worth. But true worth can only be found within themselves. They are forever stuck not realizing their actual value.

- *Fear of rejection.* This person looks for rejection. They are so afraid of being rejected that they find rejection where it does not exist. You can never call enough, text enough or do enough. There is always a reason to feel rejected. Since an argument is perceived as a rejection, the fights can be explosive.

- *Fear of responsibility.* Any type of responsibility pushes this person's button. Sadly, they cannot change anything about themselves because that requires taking responsibility. This person can't be wrong or need to change.

- *Jealousy.* See the example above. This person deals with a fear of loss. This is a mental hell. Control it or it will destroy your life.

There are many more fears. Look inside you and see if you can find any fear buttons. After a fight, go back to where it started to see if you can identify what set you off. The Bible says the truth will set you free. Once you know what sets you off, you should be able to eliminate it.

At the end of this chapter, we've provided a "fight log." By tracking your fears, the things that set off a fight, you can begin the process of eliminating fears and the fights they cause.

Here's a story to illustrate this. I once counseled a young couple and explained fear buttons. Then I gave them each small horns. I told them that the horns were their fear buttons so whenever the other person pushed their fear button, they were to honk the horn. I then told the guy to tell me what was going on. About seven seconds in, his wife honked the horn. I said, "You didn't understand me. Whenever he pushes your fear button, honk your horn." I turned back to the guy and told him to continue. He started talking again. He barely said a word and she honked the horn. I said, "No, no. You are not understanding what I am saying. Once again—whenever HE pushes YOUR fear button, honk your horn." Her face turned sour, but I told the guy to start again. He opened his mouth and she honked her horn again. He got mad and honked his horn. I said "No, No." Then they both honked their horns at me!

I had to explain to them that they should never honk the horn when their spouse pushes their fear button, because they do not the ability to push their fear button. They were the only one who could push their own fear button. Whatever your fear is, no one can push that button but you. Have you ever noticed that a friend can say the same thing your spouse said to you, and you don't get upset all. Why? Because of the fear button.

How do you deal with fear? The Bible says we deal with fear by love. First John 4:18 says that love drives out fear. You see, if love can't exist when fear is present, then fear can't exist when love is present. In the moment you feel that fear button about to be pushed, if you inject some love into the circumstance, you will find that fear goes away. For example, if you start to feel jealous, start thinking well of your spouse. Make yourself think trusting thoughts. That love will drive out the fear. If you fear being controlled, put love into the moment and allow yourself to be controlled. Love conquers all.

Here's some homework for you. Consider these questions. What fears do you think you deal with? How will you overcome these fears? How will you inject love into the moment?

Fear Fight Log

Date: _____ What triggered your fear button?
Why? How do you overcome this in the future?

Date: _____ What triggered your fear button?
Why? How do you overcome this in the future?

Date: _____ What triggered your fear button?
Why? How do you overcome this in the future?

Date: _____ What triggered your fear button?
Why? How do you overcome this in the future?

Date: _____ What triggered your fear button?
Why? How do you overcome this in the future?

CHAPTER
4

STEER THE RELATION SHIP

No Skinny Sex for Me

In our marriage, my expectations for laundry are very low. Laundry is not my wife's gift or calling. We have five kids, and that alone makes laundry a full-time job. I generally take most of my laundry out and have it cleaned. All I ask for is clean underwear and white t-shirts. You might be thinking, why not just do your own laundry? But that's the funny thing. Holly gets mad if I do my own laundry. Apparently, the only way she is happy is if no one does my laundry!

Now, the underwear is not that important to me because I can get five days out of one pair. I can turn them around, inside out, upside down (you get the picture). But I love my white t-shirts and have to have a clean one every morning. For the first five years of our marriage, I kept running out of t-shirts. So one day in my frustration, I went out to the store and bought myself enough white t-shirts so I would never run out again. I bought 45 white t-shirts! Mathematically speaking, how often would my wife have to wash t-shirts? I mean, God flooded the entire earth for 40 days, right? If she would only do laundry once every flood cycle, I would never run out!

So here it is, Day 46 since I bought the t-shirts. Who would have guessed it? I ran out of clean t-shirts. I discovered this early in the morning before work and boy was I mad! But I'm smart enough to know that you don't complain to a lady in her ninth month of pregnancy. However, I'm not smart enough to know not to talk to myself out loud. (It actually bugs me that I can't talk to myself without her listening!) As I was walking out of our bedroom talking to myself, I said, "You know, God forbid that I have a clean white t-shirt in the house."

Holly shot out of bed like there was fire in it. Then she began to let me know all of my faults. Now, I only brought up one of her faults (and even then, I did it privately), so you'd think she'd tell me only one of mine, maybe two. I will usually take a two-for-one deal. But that's not how it works. I tell her one, she tells me all. And, as I understand it, I have a lot of faults. In fact, all the problems in the world were my fault at that moment. Holly blamed me for high interest rates, increased unemployment—she even tried to pin the Kennedy assassination on me!

Five minutes later, we were up to the letter "G" on my alphabetical list of faults, and I was getting even madder. I burst out with, "All I want is clean t-shirts! You're home all day long. Throw a load of laundry in the wash before your nap. Maybe get up at ten instead of noon and put a load in!" For some reason, this made her madder—go figure. In fact, she got so mad her eyes turned black, her hair seemed to disappear into her skull, and she began shaking. I knew that whatever she said next was going to hurt. I admit, I was scared! Holly just sat there for like a minute. I felt like I was watching a bomb, just waiting for it to blow. Then she said, "I am so sick and tired of your whining and complaining! I promise you—I swear to you—you will never run out of white t-shirts again! I'm going to wash them day and night. You're going to have white t-shirts up to your eyeballs! YOU WILL NEVER RUN OUT OF WHITE T-SHIRTS AGAIN!"

I'm thinking (sarcastically) *Please, not that! Don't give me lots and lots of clean t-shirts!* But the way she said it made me so mad. For whatever reason, I yelled back, "The heck you will! Don't you go telling me that I'm going to have a lot of clean t-shirts." I walked away thinking, *There! I told her!*

A few days later, it was sharpening time again. This time, Holly made me so mad that I pulled out the secret weapon—the sex card. As I said, this is a weapon men reach for anytime they're in a fight and it looks like they might lose. They don't play that card often, but the funny thing is that when they do, they bring on a bigger fight. I mean big!

Realize that at the time all this "sharpening" was going on, Holly was nine months pregnant (I think she gave birth five days later). I hadn't seen any "action" in a long time, and it was affecting me. When I played the sex card, it looked like Holly's eyes were going to roll back in her head. Scary! But, again, she just sat there. Then she began slowly, with deliberate fury: "When I have this baby and lose all this weight, I'm going to be skinny and you're going to be having skinny sex all the time. You're going to have it in the morning, at lunchtime, dinnertime, bedtime, in the middle of the night. You will be having so much skinny sex, you won't be able to walk!" She screamed, "YOU'RE GOING TO HAVE IT UNTIL YOU BEG ME TO QUIT!" Again, I'm thinking, *Please! Don't give me lots and lots of skinny sex!* The way she said it made me mad, and for whatever reason, I responded, "The heck you will! Don't you go telling me that I'm going to have a lot of skinny sex! It will be a cold day in hell before I take skinny sex!"

If you can follow this chapter's advice, you will eliminate most of your stupid arguments.

> *"The eye is the lamp of the body. If therefore your eye is good, your whole body will be full of light. If your eye is bad, your whole body will be full of darkness."*
>
> Matthew 6:22-23

This scripture says what you choose to see determines how you feel. If you see all the things your spouse doesn't do, you will be filled with anger and bitterness. But if you can learn to see all that they do, you will be happy and excited.

Go back to when you were dating and madly in love. No matter what anyone said about your future spouse, you only saw the good. Your dad could tell you your boyfriend's faults, your friends could tell you all that was wrong with your girlfriend. But that didn't matter because all you could focus on was what you loved about them. So much so, that you decided to spend your life with them. During this time, your relationship was full of passion and excitement.

Let's fast forward to after a few years of marriage. What's the difference? Now you see the bad stuff that has always been there. The passion isn't there, the excitement is gone. Things that never bothered you before make you want to put a pillow over her face.

I just finished a series called "What's In Your Cup." I was using the example that what you percolate inside dictates the aroma that comes out of the cup. Percolate some great coffee beans, a great aroma comes out. If you cook up some sour milk, you will not have such a great aroma. What you allow to cook inside your mind will generate an aroma in your environment as well. If you spend your time thinking about all the things your wife doesn't do or things she does do that annoy you, you're "percolating." At the office, do you tell your buddies what a hag she is? If so, then by the time you get home, that aroma spills out into the home. You can try and cover it with a kiss and some kind words, but an argument is coming. Same thing for you ladies. If you cook up all the bad he does throughout the day and get on the phone and complain about him and talk about all he doesn't do, then by the time he gets home, you have crock-potted a fight waiting to happen!

I met with a young man once who had been married a few years and was considering divorce. He went into all the things his wife didn't do. Finally I interrupted him and said, "You have a horrible marriage. I have a great marriage. What do you think the difference is?"

He thought for a moment. "My wife doesn't do #$# and yours does?"

I smiled and shook my head. "Not true. My wife doesn't do number one on your list, definitely doesn't do number two through four, hasn't even thought about doing number five and number six. Well, maybe on a good week." He looked puzzled as I continued, "Does your wife love God?"

"Well, yes."

"Is she a good mother?"

"Yeah, she is a great mother."

"Is she trustworthy?"

"Of course."

"You see, I choose to look at the good things my wife is doing. I focus on her great qualities. I focus on the gift God has given me. You focus on things that simply don't matter."

Once he changed what he allowed inside, he and his wife's marriage turned around and today they are still happily married. The Bible says in I Corinthians 13 that love thinks no wrong. Every time you allow yourself to think wrong, you have stepped out of love. The Bible says we are to cast down any thought that is contrary to the Word of God. (2 Corinthians 10:5) That means that you need to fight that thought. If you have a thought that says she is a (fill in the blank), you say, "Nope, she is a blessing from God." You have to make your mind think *good.*

"Whatever is true, whatever is noble, whatever is right, whatever things are pure, whatever things are lovely, whatever things are of good report, if there is any virtue, if there is anything praiseworthy, meditate on these things."

Philippians 4:8

This means you should think only good thoughts. Do you want to get out of the emotions of anger from a fight fast? If so, just step back and go over all of the things you love about your spouse. Force your mind to think only about the good. What typically happens when you walk away after a fight that has not been reconciled? You start thinking about all the bad, and your emotions go bad as well. As soon as you start thinking about all the good, your emotions go good.

This concept isn't just for your thoughts, but also for your words—what you say to yourself and to others. Make sure you only speak good words about your spouse. The Bible says what comes out of your mouth brings life or death. It says your words are the rudder of life. This means that your words steer your life, your *Relation Ship*.

I always tell couples to speak what they want, not what they got. In time, you get what you speak. So maybe he *is* lazy. But you say, "I am blessed with such an amazing man of God. He is a doer, he is a blessing." (Of course your best friend says, "Is this the same man you've been complaining about for ten years? You find a new man?")

You need to say, "My wife is a gift from God. I love her with all of my heart. She is such a blessing to me. I am the luckiest guy in the world." *But Pastor, that's not true.* Speak it until it is true. The Bible tells us to speak those that are not as though they are. (Romans 4:17) We must speak it first, then we will see it manifest. By putting a new blend in our cup, we will change the aroma of our relationship.

Whatever is in your cup sets the mood for your home. Is your home filled with the aroma of love or bitterness? Which cup will bring you joy? Which cup will bring you fights? I challenge you to try this for one week. Make a decision that you will only allow yourself to speak good and think good about your spouse.

Of course, there's more homework for this chapter. Make a list of all the great characteristics of your spouse. If you can't come up with any, that is because you have been percolating the wrong stuff for too long. Take some time and really list out the gifts that he or she possesses. Every morning and every night, read through the list and add any new ones you discover. Any time you are angry with your spouse, break out the list and go over every item. (Warning: This will usually make you wonder why you are mad at something so stupid.)

Confess the following scriptures every day. Faith cometh by hearing, and hearing, and hearing. The more you hear how good your spouse is, the more you will believe it.

Confessions for Husbands

I love my wife with all my heart. She is my princess and the love of my life. I will lay down my life for her. Her needs are more important than mine. Today, I will do all I can to make her feel like she is the most important thing in my life. I will make her feel loved today and for the rest of our long happy lives together.

I am in love with my wife for who she is.

I will control my emotions; my emotions will not control me. I will always respond to my wife in love.

My wife is a gift from God. She is worth far more than any treasure. I thank You, God for giving her to me (Genesis 2:18).

I have full confidence in my wife and I trust her with all that I have (Proverbs 31:11).

My wife brings me good all the days of our life (Proverbs 31:12).

I walk in love so I am patient, I am kind, I do not envy, I do not boast, I am not proud. I am not easily angered; I keep no record of wrong. I walk in forgiveness. I always trust, I always give, and my love will never fail (I Corinthians 13:4-7).

I love to give my time, effort, and myself to my wife.

I treat my wife with respect and I treat her like she is the most valuable thing in my life (1 Peter 3:7).

I have found favor from the Lord, for I have found an awesome wife (Proverbs 18:22).

I will hold no grudge toward my wife. I walk in forgiveness and I never go to bed angry.

I love my wife and I am never harsh with her. I always respond to her in love (Colossians 3:19).

My wife is the workmanship of God, created in Christ Jesus to do good works, which God prepared in advance for her to do (Ephesians 2:10).

Confessions for Wives

Today, I will make my husband feel important and valuable. I will make him feel like he can accomplish anything. He is my knight in shining armor and is a gift from God.

I walk in love so I am patient, I am kind, I do not envy, I do not boast, I am not proud. I am not easily angered, I keep no record of wrong. I walk in forgiveness. I always trust, I always give, and my love will never fail (I Corinthians 13:4-7).

My husband submits himself to God. He resists the devil, and the devil flees from him. My husband draws near to God and God draws near to him (James 4:7).

I am lucky to have the man God gave me.

I will control my emotions; my emotions will not control me. I will always respond to my husband in love.

My husband is wise and understanding. He shows it by his good life and by deeds done in the humility that comes from wisdom (James 3:13).

My husband's steps are directed by the Lord (Proverbs 20:24).

I love my husband with all my heart.

My husband's faith does not rest on men's wisdom but on God's power (1 Corinthians 2:5).

My husband gives gentle answers which turn away wrath (Proverbs 15:1).

My husband trusts in the Lord with all his heart and leans not on his own understanding. In all his ways he acknowledges God and God makes his path straight (Proverbs 3:5).

My husband loves me.

My generous husband will prosper and while he gives to others, he himself will be given to (Proverbs 11:25).

My husband obeys and serves God, and we will spend the rest of our days in prosperity and our years in contentment (Job 36:11).

I am a wise woman; I build my house and it prospers (Proverbs 14:1).

I am a wife of noble character and I am a crown to my husband.

I watch over the affairs of the household with excellence (Proverbs 31:27).

I bring my husband good all the days of my life (Proverbs 31:12).

My husband loves me as he loves himself, and I love him (Ephesians 5:33).

My husband loves me and is not harsh with me (Colossians 3:19).

I will speak nothing but good about my husband in my words and thoughts.

I hold no grudge nor will I allow myself to stay mad at my husband.

I walk in forgiveness, never going to bed angry.

THE POWER OF LOVE

One of my great joys in life is getting my wife's phone when I'm alone and messing with it. Usually, I send texts to her friends and family members from her phone. Sometimes, I say some off the wall stuff like "I have this crazy onion looking thing growing on my feet, any ideas?" or "I have a small patch of hair growing in the center of my back. Do you think this will affect swim suit season?"

You get the idea. After a while, her friends catch on and respond, Hahaha, Scot!" One day, I found her phone lying on the counter and I grabbed it and thought of a great idea. I went into her calendar and every Tuesday at 1p.m., I scheduled "Make Love to Scot". This was so funny. Not knowing, of course, that all my kids share the same iTunes account with her. My 11th grader's phone went off in English class and he looks at it to find out he has a reminder. Even Holly thought she put it in there which makes me feel worse knowing she has to schedule that time with me.

"Come on honey! If you schedule something, you need to make it a priority!"

"*What about me? What about my needs? I feel empty! I'm drained!*" These are common statements we have all heard, spoken or thought in our marriages. We all have needs, and there is nothing wrong with having needs, nor is it selfish. We have a love tank, and it is very difficult to give when our tank is running on empty. But what is more important than our needs? Meeting our spouse's needs. If I fill my wife's tank up, she fills my tank up, and we both run on full. If I try and take to get my tank full, and she tries to take to get her tank full, we both battle on empty.

> "*Whoever refreshes others will be refreshed.*"
>
> Proverbs 11:25

If you spend time refreshing your spouse, you in turn will feel refreshed. It's that whole sowing and reaping thing. Give what you want and in time, you will receive what you desire.

God put some natural triggers in man/woman so that when our needs are met, we desire to meet our spouse's needs. This takes us back to the idea that you have to change what you have the power to change. (That would be *you*.) Later in the book we will discuss what to do when the other person is not meeting your needs, but for now, let's focus on changing ourselves.

Most of the time the problem isn't that our spouse isn't trying to meet our needs, but rather that they have no real clue what our needs are. Add to that the fact that *we don't even know what our own real needs are*. Because of this, we fight for things that just aren't important. In the next few chapters, we will be going over the needs of the man and the woman. It's exciting how God created man and woman to need each other and for our needs to complement each other. It is in the meeting of each other's needs that we truly become one.

Let's start by looking at two very basic needs. We won't spend a lot of time on this, but these things are good to know. First, we all have a need for great relationships. Think about the best times of your life and the worst. Both probably centered around relationships. The need to connect with others is in our DNA. God created us to develop great relationships. We will never live life at the level of happiness our Creator intended for us to have until we do what we were created to do. The Bible, cover-to-cover, is about relationships. When they asked Jesus to sum up His view of life, He said, "Love God, love others, love yourself."

Second, we need to love. I realize this is another basic need (the next ones will be new and cool), but let's not forget that life is about love. First Corinthians 13 says that without love we are nothing. We can be successful but without love, we have a wasted life. We can see this on the cover of magazines. The super-successful actor is strung out on drugs. He has it all, but he is missing LOVE.

Life is best when you are loving. Remember, love drives out fear. It drives out the root of all negative emotions. Love brings hope and faith, the root of all positive emotions.

I'm not talking about the world's definition of love. Their love comes and goes like seasons. I'm talking about God's love. First Corinthian 13:4-8 says that love is patient, love is kind, it does not envy (*Her life is so much easier;*

He has it a lot better than me), it doesn't boast (*Look at all I do; I'm the best in the relationship*). Love is not proud, it does not dishonor (*He's such a jerk; She's such a hag*). Love is not self-seeking *(What about my needs?)*. It is not easily angered, keeps no record of wrong (*How many fights do we bring up what happened a long, long time ago?*), does not delight in evil, but rejoices with the truth. Love always protects, always trusts, always hopes and always perseveres. LOVE NEVER FAILS.

Notice how God's love is not a feeling. It is something you do. Love is a verb, not an adjective (little Gilbert High English coming at you). The world says love is something that comes and goes. They say things like, "I fell out of love with her." Biblically (and grammatically!) that makes no sense. Let me give you an example. Let's use "run," another verb. If I want to "feel run," I need to what? I need to run. If I run, I feel out of breath, my heart starts pounding. *I feel run.* If I want to feel love, then I need to do what? Basic reasoning says that I need to love.

What if I said to you that I no longer "feel run" for Holly? Even though you don't have a physical education degree, you would be able to tell me what to do to "feel run" with her. It's simple. I just need to run with her. If I run with her, I will "feel run." You might say, "I fell out of run with her." Here's an easy fix: Start running with her.

So when someone says, "I no longer love her," I say "Yes!" and *that* is the problem.

"I know it's the problem, that's why I'm leaving her."

"That would be loving her even less. What you need to do is love her."

"But I don't."

"I know, and that is the problem. What you need to do is love her."

"You are not hearing me! I don't LOVE HER!"

"Exactly, and that is the problem. You need to start loving her."

"I want to hit you in the face right now!"

"I, too, would love to hit you in the face." (Actual counseling session I had with a guy.)

For homework, read that scripture from Proverbs and I Corinthians after every fight, then look at what you could have done differently. Next time, inject some godly love into the moment and drive out that FEAR!

CHAPTER
6

MOST IMPORTANT NEED
OF A WOMAN

No Potato Salad for You

So here we are. Mother's Day is coming up and I always like to make Mother's Day special because I have the most amazing wife! She is the best mom. I also have an amazing mom and she has an amazing mom. So I really try and make Mother's Day special for all the ladies. Last year, I spent $300 just on the meal at a fancy hotel.

This year, Holly came to me (that is important, she *came to me* with this idea for Mother's Day), saying rather than spend time driving, waiting for a table, and going through all the hassle of going out to eat, why not have a BBQ at the house? My man-heart did a back flip with excitement. Right away, my man-mind began to do some complex math about the money I would be saving. I thought, *I have to go pick up hot dogs, hamburgers, potato chips, maybe I will spring for some baked beans. It will be an amazing, magical, little Mother's Day.* Quickly, I figured 20 burgers and buns would run $25, hotdogs (the cheap ones) and buns $15, chips and drinks $20, beans and miscellaneous accessories $20. This was going to cost me around $100. God is good! I just made $200! Right away, with a smile like a kid with an ice cream cone, I said "I am going to the store to pick up the stuff."

Holly responded. "Okay, well let me give you a list of things that you need to pick up." This made me a little annoyed because I'm not some barbeque newbie. But it was Mother's Day, so I shook it off and listened to her. Holly began by saying, "You need hamburgers, hot dogs" (*Come on woman challenge me*). She continued: "I don't want your cheap hotdogs" (*ouch, that hurt a little*), I want the Hebrew Nationals and I want the bakery buns." I felt a slight pinch to my heart, but my mind said, well that's only an extra $20; we're still doing great. "Then we will need some steaks for the adults. Better get eight of them." I felt like someone just hit me in the stomach. I wanted to scream, "Do you know how much a steak costs? Like six bucks a steak—that's an extra fifty dollars." I gritted out a smile, reminding myself it *was* Mother's Day. "You know what, get our older two boys a steak, too."

Without thinking, I responded, "Nope, they can eat a $5 hotdog." As soon as I said this, the air in the room seemed to change.

"It's Mother's Day, make it special! Get them a steak! (This cut me a little; I always make it special.) Get them a steak."

I could feel my face getting redder, but I just smiled and said, "Ok, but I don't want a steak." *(Of course, I love steak more than most anything in life.)*

"But you love steak," she replied.

But I stuck to my guns and said, "Sick of them. No steak for me."

You will find out why in this chapter, but Holly's subconscious began to go to work. She was now going to force me to love her.

She continued, "That's fine, we need to have some chicken."

I'm thinking, *Oh my gosh, chicken too.* I blurted out, "Everybody is going to have a steak. They don't need chicken. Why are we killing so many animals for your meal?"

Let's pause to see what is happening. Basically I am saying she is not worthy of steak and chicken. I am digging my feet in. Why? From earlier chapters we know this is my fear in action. Fear of being controlled. I am acting like a crazy man at this point.

Now it's time for her to deliver the fatal blow. "I want snow crab." She paused for effect. "I want five pounds of snow crab." At this point, it took nearly everything in me to just compose myself and not run out of the room screaming. The anger boiled. I could feel steam trying to escape. I gathered my last bit of self-control and replied, "Sounds good." It felt like I spat the words out.

Another pause. With a smarmy smile she said, "I want you to make homemade potato salad." Even today, this statement hits me hard. Understand this: In my lifetime, I have never made potato salad. I have never boasted of making potato salad. Going back five generations, I can

confidently say not one of my relatives has ever made potato salad. No one in Holly's family has made potato salad.
None of us have ever eaten homemade potato salad. This
was the craziest request of all time. It was her test of my
love. And I failed miserably!

I felt a snap in my soul. I looked her in the eyes and
through gritted teeth said, "Please hear my words. As long
as I live and continuing on into eternity, I will never make
you potato salad. If getting into heaven now requires me
making you potato salad, I will gladly burn in hell before
you get a single bite of my potato salad! If saving a loved
one meant making potato salad, I would let them die!"
This turned into, what I would say, was our biggest fight
ever! This epic fight illustrates the most important need of
a woman.

Let's get into the needs most people don't know about
or don't fully understand. So far, we've talked about two
needs— relationships and love. We're going to talk about
other needs. If you get only one of these needs, this is the
one. We will break this one up into female then male. Both
are found in the marriage scriptures in Ephesians.

Woman's Most Important Need:

*"Husbands, love your wives, just as Christ loved the
church and gave himself up for her."*

Ephesians 5:25

Let's first talk about how Christ loved the church. Does
Christ's love for the church depend upon what the church
does for Him? Does the church have to change anything to

receive His love? No! Christ loves the church unconditionally. He loves the church because it exists. He says you don't need to change a thing.

A woman's most important need is to be loved for who she is without needing to change a single thing. God put a need in her to be loved because she exists. A woman's greatest desire is for a man to lay down his life for her, *even if she changes nothing.* She wants to be the most important thing in his world. Men, if your wife sees that she is the most important thing in your world, she will find you irresistible.

Let's go all the way back to when she was six years old. She played princess, waiting in a tower for her prince to save her. She knew her prince would come and slay the dragon, not because she is a great cook, not because she cleans a great house, but because she exists. She wants a prince to lay down his life, and slay the dragon for her. Now, grown up, she wants to know she is the most important thing in your life, and that you will give it all up for her.

First Peter 3:7 says that a husband should treat his wife with understanding, giving honor (that word means treat her as if she had high value—the way you would treat a new Ferrari), as to the fragile vessel (like really expensive fine china), and as being heirs together that your prayers may not be hindered. That last part of this verse hit me hard. I wonder how many men aren't getting their prayers answered because of how they are treating God's baby girl. Let's be honest, how my boys are treated is a lot different than how I treat my daughter. Boys get hurt and are told, "Walk it off." My princess gets hurt, well, someone has to answer for that. *I wonder how hurting His little girl goes over with Him.*

Needless to say, this scripture says to treat your wife as if she is the most valuable thing you have. Proverbs says she is worth more than treasure.

"*Scot, she doesn't do this and she doesn't do that. Scot, when she starts meeting my needs, I will meet hers. When she changes I will change.*" These are all things I have heard many times. But watch what happens when you love her because she exists. When you meet her most important need:

> "*Husbands, love your wives, just as Christ also loved the church and gave Himself up for her. That He might sanctify and cleanse her with the washing of water by the word, that He might present her to himself a glorious church, not having spot or wrinkle, or any such thing, but that she should be holy and without blemish.*
>
> Ephesians 5:25

As you love your wife unconditionally, it changes her. Before long, she is holy without blemish (she is perfect)! You have been trying to change her for how many years? Change you. Love her (I Corinthians 13:4), make her feel like she is the most important person in the world. Then step back and watch as she becomes an amazing wife!

When a woman is not getting this need met, she will subconsciously fight to get this need met. This means that if you won't lay down your life, she will fight to take your life away. But if you lay your life down, she will always give it back. To a man's mind, this sounds crazy, but when you truly understand this need, it makes so much sense.

For example, Holly would often call me in the middle of the day while I was at work. I would be in the middle of a staff meeting with 27 staff members. She'd say, "Hi, what are you doing?"

I would respond by saying, "Sitting here with my staff having a meeting."

Let's pause here. For any other person in the world, she would now say, "You're busy. Let me call you back." That makes sense, right? Not when you are talking about her most important need. Instead, Holly would start a light conversation, saying something like, "What do you want for dinner? I was thinking tater-tot casserole, but well, hold on—let me see if we have any tater tots." All the while, my entire staff was staring at me as I just sat on the phone listening to my wife.

Then she resumed the conversation, "No tater tots. What do you think about soup cheese crisp night? Hey that reminds me, I was talking to Kelly yesterday while we were heading to Target. No, wait. We were heading toward Walmart. I think. Maybe it was Target. I guess it doesn't matter. So I was telling her about our trip."

At this point, I always want to take my pen and jam it into my stomach like a great samurai. It takes all of my control not to yell out, "WHO CARES! I'M IN A MEETING!" But I don't want to fight, so I take a deep breath and calmly and as lovingly as I can, say, "Honey, I'm in a staff meeting. Can I call you back?" Now for any other person in the world, this would be fine. But not for me. She yells, "OH, IF YOU DON'T WANT TO TALK TO ME, FINE!!!" and hangs up on me. Then I just sit there in the meeting, full of this wonderment feeling like I've been kicked in the gut. I'm in a meeting! How freaking rude is it to all these people? To a man, this makes no sense at all. She is crazy! But when you understand your wife's needs, you realize that she subconsciously wants to be important—the most important thing in your life. Your wife may not even know that she is doing this or why she is doing this. And it's not her fault—it's yours.

Once I discovered this, when Holly called me at work, I would say, "Hi beautiful, what you doing?"

She would respond, "Calling you. What are you doing?"

"Nothing as fun as talking to you."

"No really, what are you doing?"

"Just in a staff meeting. So how's your day?" I smile while I say it.

Pause. "Well, go do your staff meeting. I can call you later."

"No, you are more important than my staff meeting." I smile.

"No, just call me when you're done. Love you, bye."

The first time this happened, I literally said, "What in the world?" This makes no sense to the average man. All I had to do was give up my staff meeting for her, and she gave it back. But as long as I fought for it, she wanted it.

Here's another example. Take the guy whose wife will never let him go out golfing with his friends. When he manages to sneak away, it is always a huge fight. Why? Because she feels like golf and his friends are more important to him than she is. He should say, "I don't need any friends. You are my only friend." Then he should hang out with just her around the house for a few days. She will be like, "Stop smothering me! Go golfing or something. I need some space." As soon as you give up the friends for her, she'll give them back to you.

Another problem in many marriages is mother-in-laws. I have the greatest mom in the world, and I am proud to say I'm a momma's boy. However, this posed huge problems in the early years of our marriage. The subject of my mom always turned into this huge fight. One day I said, "Honey, I don't need her. You're the only woman for me. Let's move away so it is just you and me."

"Don't be mean—she is your mom," Holly responded. Once again, she just wanted to know she was the most important thing in my life. If she starts to feel like something else is, she will subconsciously try and take it away. But if you give it up, she will give it back.

Men, this is life changing right here. You will end up giving up anyway. After hours, days of fighting, you finally give up, so why not do it in the beginning? It's like I tell my kids, "You're going to end up doing your chores anyway. If you do the chores without being asked, you get a thank you. If you don't, we get upset *and you have to do them anyway.* So you might as well do them before we ask." Men, if you don't lay down your life, she will nag the life out of you. Ladies, I don't say that to be mean, it's in your DNA and there is nothing wrong with you wanting to be first in your husband's life.

I love how Holly will subconsciously hint to me about laying down my life for her. Men, if you miss these moments, she'll get annoyed, though she won't know why. But we know why.

Here's another example. I will be in bed waiting for Holly and she will come into the room just about to climb in bed and say, "I'm thirsty." Any man might think, *Well, go get a drink. That's what I do when I'm thirsty.* But now, you know she is saying, "Do you love me enough to drag your backside out of bed and go downstairs to get me a drink?" It's a test of love. Most of us men miss it. Before, I might have said, "Great. While you're down there, get me a drink too." Then I'd wonder why she came to bed a little annoyed. And forget trying to get pancakes. (Pancakes is our word for makin' love. Which is awkward when my six year old hears me say to Holly, "I sure could use some pancakes." Savvy screams out, "I want pancakes toooo!")

Men, learn to listen for little signs. When Holly says, "After dinner, I need to take the trash out," I used to think, *and the floors could use a good mopping too.* Now I say, "Let me take out the trash."

CHAPTER
7

TEN WAYS TO VALUE THE OL' BALL AND CHAIN

Flip Flops in Greece

Holly and I planned a trip to Greece for our 20-year anniversary. This is a big trip for a couple with five kids. Being gone ten days takes a lot of preparation, which can be quite stressful. I can understand why Holly was so annoyed. I mean, she was trying to pack for the five kids, as well as herself. She was also trying to get the schedule set up for who's taking the kid to school at eight, who's taking the kid at nine, who's picking up the kids at eleven, who's picking up the kids at three, who's picking up the kids at four, who's doing the piano practice, and who's doing the dance practice? Who's doing the wrestling practice? Who's doing the gymnastics practice? She was busy trying to orchestrate all of these things while I was busy just packing for myself. We were both really, really busy!

I also dealt with the travel company. That was my part. I'm not going to tell you the name of the company, because I don't like to badmouth, but I'm fairly certain that they don't have anyone who speaks English working for them. This helps explain some of my frustration. I thought, *this is too big of a trip to book online, so I'll give them a call.* Yet, it took four hours and five non-English speaking salespeople to get things right! So here I was, the day before we were supposed to leave, going over the itinerary. They had us flying to London then ten days later, they would fly us from Crete to Athens, then to London and then home. I don't know if you see the problem. There was no initial flight to get us from London to Crete!

I spoke with a lady who knows seventeen English words, trying to explain my problem. "Now, you understand that you have me going to London."

She's said, "Yes."

I said, "But how did I get to Crete?"

"I do not know, but you have flight home."

"That's great," I said. "I love having a flight home. The problem is, I won't be able to fly home if I'm not in Crete."

"Why are you not in Crete?"

"Because my plane doesn't make it to Crete."

"It does. You're flying home."

"I know I'm flying home, but how did I get to Crete?"

She said, "How would I know?"

I screamed with laughter at this statement. "That's my point exactly: How would you know? So you see, we have a problem."

"It looks like we do!"

"What do we do?"

She's replied, "I don't know."

So now it's an hour before we were to be picked up for the airport, and Holly and I are battling. Holly walked by and saw my Vans (my tennis shoes) on the floor. Understand this about me, I wear three different types of shoes: dress shoes, vans or flip flops. That is the full extent of what Scotty wears. Now, Holly knows that I have one pair of tennis shoes. She picked them up and said, "Are you not taking your Vans?"

Now when she said this, I thought, *Oh my God, I forgot to pack my Vans! I need my Vans, because we're gonna be walking around a lot, and doing a lot of tourist thing! I desperately need Vans. I can't walk over there in flip flops the whole time!* This all went through my mind.

But the way she said it annoyed me. Can I say that? Then, before I had a chance to answer, she said, "I don't wanna walk around Greece with a hobo in flip flops." I didn't do well with that. (My fear button— I hate to be controlled.) So I started acting crazy. I made one of my silly stupid promises and what makes it even stupider is, I live by those promises. I looked at the love of my life and said, "I'm gonna make you a promise right now. Not only am I not gonna pack the Vans, I will not wear a single tennis shoe. Nothing outside of a flipflop will be on my feet for our entire ten days in Crete."

She said, "Fine!"

I said, "Fine!"

And off we went to Crete. No Vans, no tennis shoes. We had an amazing time in Crete. Not a single fight. We laughed, had so much fun, lots of pancakes, lots of great memories. But because we walked many miles through the landscape and the terrain of Crete, I had blisters on my poor little flip flop feet.

Holly asked, "How are the flip flops?"

I said, "Great! I don't know why more people don't walk around in these all the time, they're so comfortable! I'm actually glad these are all I brought." *I would not give her the satisfaction of knowing just how bad my feet hurt.*

Day nine in Crete. We were going to a little village to do some shopping. What made this day different? It was the coldest day in Crete in *history* for this time of year. Until this point, every day was 70-75 degrees—all day long! I don't think it even got below 70 at night. I mean, it was best weather I've ever experienced. On this day, however, they had the biggest one-day change in weather history. A 40 degree change! The temperature dropped from 75 degrees to 35. I had a jacket and pants—and my flip flops.

While driving to go to our little village for shopping, the tour guide got up and said, "Hey, I have exciting news for all of you! Instead of going to the village to shop, we are going to go on a hike to an avocado farm!"

I want you to let that settle in a little bit. I had paid for an excursion to go to a village and shop. They thought a comparable substitution was a hike to see avocados. Imagine buying tickets to go to Disneyland and instead, they take you on a seven mile hike to Bed, Bath and Beyond! They're not even the same thing! I would never pay to hike to a stupid farm. The bus pulled up in the middle of nowhere, Crete, and the tour guide said, "Out!" So, we all got out and the bus drove away.

We now had to hike down mountain terrain. There were mountain goats, and I was in flip flops, hiking to an avoca-

do farm. Then we got the pleasure of
hiking back up the mountain. Look at
the picture. I may be smiling, but know
this: I was not happy. Funny what a
Fear Button will cause you to do!

In the last chapter, we talked about
a woman's most important need to be
loved for who she is. Men, here are ten
ways to show her she is the most important thing in your life:

1. **Chivalry:** Yes, the woman's movement was awesome and important. But it is sad that some parts of chivalry died with it. Men should open their wives' car door, not
because the woman can't, but because it shows the world
how valuable she is. Kings don't open their own door, because they are important. The same with you ladies. Men,
we should carry their books, bags and suitcases when we
travel. Carry in the groceries (don't let her help). We are
showing the world (and our wives) what priceless pieces of
fine china you are.

Once, Holly and I were walking out of Walmart and saw
a mom with three young kids pushing a cart full of stuff.
She looked withered and beaten down. She was on her last
nerve. As she approached the curb, a van pulled up. In the
driver seat sat a man who, based on his apparent age, had
to be her husband. She loaded the kids in the van and then
retreated to the back of the vehicle with the cart. He popped
the hatch from the driver's seat for her. Wow, too kind.

The principle of chivalry extends to other cultural rit-
uals. For example, I've always thought that, in themselves,
flowers are a waste of money. Why are flowers important?

Because they show the world how important your wife is to you. When a woman gets flowers, does she hide them under her desk? No, she displays them so the world can see how valuable she is to someone. "Did you see my flowers? Oh, are my flowers blocking your view?" In this, she is saying, "I am valuable."

Do you see how big this need is? Why does she want a diamond ring? Once again—what a waste of money. Ask any man! To her, though, the diamond represents how important she is.

Think about your wedding day. Was the wedding at all about the groom? If grooms had their way, there would be no ceremony. That day is about the whole world seeing her value.

Chivalry is men looking for ways to show the world how important your wife is to you. My rule is, I want to be the man that makes other men upset because their wives are constantly saying, "Why can't you be more like Scot?" If Holly is on a girls' getaway, I send a big basket of flowers. Then, I show up with coffees for all the ladies from Starbucks. I make the other husbands mad, but if it gets me crazy pancakes, I'm okay with that! Men, make your wife feel priceless.

On a side note, it is *so* important for your children to see how important their mom is. You can eliminate some of the teenage disrespect to Mom if Dad's example teaches them how valuable she is. My boys are trained young to open Mom's door and carry her stuff. Mom is Dad's most valuable treasure, and all my household will treat her that way.

Once, Holly was upstairs calling down to my oldest, who was fifteen at the time. He was at the test-the-water stage of maturity. How far can I take my attitude? Laken couldn't understand what Holly was saying and Holly was frustrated by his lack of response. Holly let out a final shout, "LAKEN!"

Laken, in a heat of frustration, screamed, "WHAT, WHAT, WHAT IN THE HECK DO YOU WANT?"

I was in the kitchen about 20 feet away from her. I slammed the refrigerator door, and took after Laken like a rhino charging. "What did you say to MY WIFE?" Notice, it's not Holly, it's not mom, it was *my wife*. I would never put up with a stranger talking to her that way, I sure as heck was not going to allow some fifteen year-old to talk to the love of my life like that.

Laken, seeing the beast charging at him, began to scream, "SORRY MOM! SORRY MOM!"

I got in his face and said, "You will never talk to my wife that way again!"

"Yes, Dad, yes, I understand." Now, do *you* understand? Perhaps you'll say that your wife isn't valuable. She doesn't do this and that. As I have been saying, treat her as valuable, and she will become valuable. Treat her as priceless and she will become priceless. As the farmer knows, you always have to sow before you can reap.

2. **First fruits**: If she is the most important part of your world, that means she gets the first and best of your time. Get up a little bit early in the morning to get her coffee. Spend the first part of your day finding about what she has going on and sharing your day. She is worth it. When you get home at night, tell the kids to go play. Spend the first twenty minutes sharing your day with her and let her share hers. Turn off your cell phone. If you are talking to

her and glancing at your phone, this says she is not first in your life. Turn off the television and all other distractions. Make it all about her. You will be surprised how much happier your wife will be if you just do this.

"Scot, I'm not a good communicator." I have an idea; become one. It's not hard. Just ask her about her day, look into her eyes and really listen. Nod once in a while. Then add some stuff from your day. She doesn't care how interesting it is, just that you are engaged in conversation. In that moment, nothing else matters except for what she has to say. Pretend she is Jesus telling you the secrets of the world, and listen.

3. **Date Night**: She is your world. Why wouldn't you want to take her out like you used to before you had kids? Men, it is your job to make sure you have a date with her every week. You make it happen. You need to fight for it. It shows her how important the relationship is to you.

I find that a majority of young marriages that are on the brink of divorce are missing date nights. In many cases, the couple has a young child. Their world centers on the child. That is very unhealthy. The world needs to revolve around the marriage, not around the child. The husband/wife relationship is the most important relationship in the home.

Think about it. Many of us came from a broken home. What would you have given if Mom and Dad would just have gotten along? Mom and Dad's relationship is the nucleus of the home. All other relationships get their security from the marriage bond. If the marriage is doing great, the children gain security and confidence. If Mom and Dad are not doing great, insecurity and emotional issues take root. *A great marriage is the greatest gift you can give any child.*

So when you're wringing your hands over time away from the kids, remember: A date with your wife is a great gift to your children. Don't have the money? You didn't have the money when you were dating, but you found it. Sell your golf clubs, cancel cable television. Find the money. She is that important. Your date doesn't have to be expensive. My parents had no money, so they picnicked at the park or split a dessert at Denny's.

The focus of the date must be the relationship. With that in mind, going out with other couples does not count as a date. Double-dating is fun and you should do it if you can, but only if you also have a date night that week. A date is not just a movie. Movies aren't relationship time. Dinner and a movie is perfect as long as you engage in conversation at dinner. Staying home is *never* a date. Every night together should end at home. On date night, she needs to get out of the house. No kids, no laundry, no pressures.

4. **Trips**: Twice a year, plan a getaway. These trips don't have to be expensive. You don't have to travel far. The trip can be as simple as a hotel up the road for two nights. Your relationship has to have this and a getaway makes her feel like she is important to you. The two of you will come back refreshed.

You'll come back as better parents, too. That's important. But remember, one day the kids will be gone and all you will have is the two of you. Your marriage is the foundational relationship. If you don't put time into it, it will crumble. I don't want to wake up one morning in my sixties having to start over with a new marriage because I didn't invest time in the marriage I have now.

5. **Protect her**: I don't mean this in a weird, fearful way, but be concerned for her well-being. If she is driving at night or out and about, show your concern. If your Ferrari was out, you would have concerns. Same for the most important person in your life.

Make sure your kids treat your wife with honor and respect. If someone keyed your Ferrari, you would be all over that. Same thing for your wife. My kids better never talk disrespectfully to the queen of my world. She is the love of my life, and all will treat her as such.

This protective attitude shows her how valuable she is to you. A simple, "I hate it when you have to drive at night" can go a long way. How about an occasional, "It's late. Let me run to the store for you." She might get annoyed and say, "I'm a big girl!" but deep down, you are meeting a need.

6. **Talk "good" about her**. Talk about your wife like you are describing your awesome Ferrari. Don't allow yourself to fall into that "man talk" about the "ol' ball and chain." She is God's greatest gift to you. Let the world know. This idea applies to speaking to yourself about her as well. Say and think nothing but good about her. You will surprised how much this alone will change you.

Remember that during a fight is the most important time to speak good of the love of your life. If you can't defend her to yourself, you will never be able to defend her to the world. Be that knight in shining armor who slays the dragon of negative thoughts and words.

7. **Show her affection**: Fight to hold her hand, to touch her. You want her by you on the couch, in the movies. Kiss her goodbye, hold and hug her tight. Don't let a night go by that you don't fight to touch her all night long.

Make her feel like her touch is so very important to you. Studies show that people who have regular physical contact are a lot happier. You were made to love and to touch. Make her feel like she is so valuable, so important, that you need her by you. She is your air, and you suffocate without her.

8. **Divorce is not an option**: Often times in a fight, we throw out things like, "Maybe we should call it quits" or "Maybe this isn't working." There are words said in the heat of the moment. You have to realize that women are the soil, we are the seed. Those words get planted, and they will bring forth a harvest. Remember, she wants a man who will fight for her. She may say, "Maybe we should call it quits," but she doesn't mean it. Subconsciously, she wants her prince to say, "No way, we are together forever." I have gotten out of more fights by that comment alone. "Honey, there is nothing you could do to make me quit you." She is priceless. Fight for her.

Men, when you do say divorce or hint at divorce, that seed just lays there in the soil. I like to say a woman "crock pots" those words. She lets those things come to a slow simmer. The thought makes her feel worthless, like something that you could easily discard. You won't fight for her? She begins to subconsciously disconnect from the relationship. Then one day, she leaves and the man wonders, "What happened?"

9. **Gifts**: Gifts show her and those around her how truly valuable she is. Now, most moms will say things like, "Let's spend the money on the kids," but your kids need to see how valuable your wife is to you. Sure, money might be tight. But think ahead, save your work over time, and get the most important person in your world something special.

"Well Scot, it's not about the gift, it's the thought." That is what cheap people say to ease their conscience. I'm not saying spend a grand on Christmas, but I am saying that whatever you spend on the kids, you spend more on her. Like it or not, your kids are watching. And the gift puts a value on your relationship. Your kids may want more, but they need to see how important Mom is. Your goal is for her to go, "WOW, you spent too much! You put too much thought into this." She'll be wrong, of course. I could never spend too much on the greatest gift I have ever received.

10. **Tell her she's important:** This last one is simple. And if you're doing the other nine things, she'll believe you when you tell her.

Is IHOP a Man's Most Important Need?

I'm the Scorpion King

At one time, our house had a scorpion infestation. We killed five to ten scorpions a day. I woke up one day at 5 am. (What follows is my perception of this early morning and may not be completely what happened, but this is how I saw it.) I hopped out of bed and began looking for my pants. Of course, they were right where they were supposed to be, crumpled up on the floor. I put one leg in and as I pushed my leg through, the bottom of my pants did that little whip thing. At that moment, something the size of a puppy snapped out the end of the pant leg. It let out a Godzilla *schreeeeeech!* When it landed on the floor (with a thud), its massive tail whipped around and struck the air as it charged toward me. You could hear each massive foot *ching* on the floor. It sounded like pins dropping.

Here is an interesting fact about me that you probably didn't know. I didn't know it either at the time. I guess I scream like a six-year-old girl if a scorpion is charging at me. I let out a scream my daughter would have been proud of. My wife rolled over and said, "What in the world is going on?" But I didn't have time to answer her foolishness as I had a Revelation 12 Beast charging at me!

At that point, I was vulnerable. I had one leg in my pants and no shoes on my feet. I frantically began to search the room for a weapon. Finally, my eye caught something on my nightstand—my Bible. I grabbed it and with both hands, I smashed it to the floor. The creature seemed to simply catch the Bible effortlessly overhead. I panicked and began to jump up and down on the Word of God until I heard the sweet pop and gush of victory. (I got a new Bible after that.) There I stood on the Bible, sweat pouring down my face. I was out of breath, but I had a small sense of victory after slaying that beast.

My wife's voice snapped me out of my triumphant trance. "What in the world is going on?"

I paused for effect. "I was putting on my pants and a scorpion shot out the leg."

The love of my life, my wife for over 22 years didn't say, "OMG, are you all right?" She didn't say, "I hope you are fine." She just casually said, "That's why you don't leave your pants on the floor!" She then rolled over and went back to sleep.

Was she saying that the fact that I'm a slob was the reason for the attack? If it was a thousand years ago and I killed a dragon, would it have also been my fault? And what about the vicious monster I vanquished?

A woman needs to be valued for WHO SHE IS. A man, on the other hand, needs to be valued for WHAT HE DOES. Do you see how God put it all together? I do for her, and she values what I do. This way, we both have our most important need met.

Ephesians 5:33 says the wife must respect her husband. That word "respect" can also be translated as honoring or valuing his work. In other words, value his efforts in what he does. Women love movies where the princess is saved. Men like *Brave Heart*, where the man goes out and conquers for his lady.

Women, if you can make your husband feel valuable for what he does, he will find you irresistible. He will do more for you than you could ever imagine. He will become an unstoppable force of success. If you put him down and make him feel useless, he will become that. In a way, you are the rudder of his success. Sure, there are lazy guys out there and no matter what you do, they won't do anything. But most of the time, a lazy guy just needs a woman to believe in him.

Ladies, my grandpa always said, "You can kick a mule, beat a mule, but a mule won't move. But if you can *convince* a mule to move, now that is how you get work done." Beating your man down will never work, but convince him, entice him, encourage him, and I believe you can get any man to move.

If a man had his way, his trophies would all be in the front room. The heads of all the animals he has slain would be hanging in the living room for all to see and admire. *Let the world see what I have accomplished. I am a great warrior.*

The first time Holly came over to my house, I had taken the better part of the day to shine all of my trophies. I arranged them so the bigger, cooler ones stood out. I had a whole shelf of my life's accomplishments on display, ready to be fawned over. When Holly walked in, she said, "Nice room," and then walked out.

"Wait! Check out this trophy from fourth grade city baseball champ. What about MVP wrestler 1987 (see how I slid that in the book)? Come on! Look at this one, participation in third grade crafts! OMG, I am super sexy and cool. I have done great things, thus I am a great catch! Why are you not in total amazement at what I have done?"

I tried to establish my value through my accomplishments because that's how men feel valued. For example, if you and your spouse go to a party at someone's house, the ladies scurry off to talk about who they are. But what do the men do? They say, "Hey, come check out the barbeque I built. Check out the buck I shot." We go and talk about what we have done. It is our most important need, to be valued for what we do.

Look at how men and women communicate. I can go on a fishing trip with a buddy for three days. When I come home, I want to tell Holly all about the fish I caught, how I got a bigger fish than Pete (made up name). Somewhere toward the end of the conversation, I mention how Pete and his wife are breaking up. She wonders why. I say, "Don't know. Guess they don't get along."

She would inquire, "But you were with him three days and you didn't ask why? How is he doing? Is he depressed, angry?"

I stammer. "I don't know. Guess he's alright, he didn't mention anything. He caught some good fish though."

Holly then calls his wife and afterward shares the details of her conversation for an hour and a half—how she feels, what she is going through, etc. Honestly, I just wanted to talk about the cool fish I caught.

It like the knight who comes back after slaying the dragon and says, "Look at what I have done!" as he swings the dragon's head.

The Princess says, "So how did it feel to kill the dragon? What were you going through?"

"Ahhhh, don't know. I just wanted to kill the dragon and maybe get a kiss. Hopefully some pancakes later."

Then the next thing you know, the knight and the princess are in a stupid argument. All because they don't understand each other's needs.

CHAPTER
9

TEN WAYS TO MAKE HIM FEEL VALUABLE FOR WHAT HE DOES

Before we go into this, I want this illustration to hit home. It will truly give you a picture of men and women. Men are like dogs and women are like cats. According to a man, cats are unpredictable. One second, they want to be touched, but two seconds later, they hiss at you. When you want to play, they want to be alone. When you want to be alone, they want to play. You can never tell what a cat is thinking. They want you to cater to their every need. Their emotions are very heightened. It's either a purr or a hiss—and it can change in a blink of an eye!

When you are busy, the cat wants your attention. When you want to give it attention, it's busy. You can't train a cat to do tricks. A cat does what it wants to do. It leaves hair everywhere.

It doesn't like to be told "good cat" when they do what they are told. Actually, it doesn't do what it's told. It chooses when it wants to be touched. A cat is very concerned with its appearance. Cats won't get in the pool because it will ruin their hair. Cats cost you an arm and a leg!

A dog, according to a woman, lies around all day, sprawled on the most comfortable piece of furniture. It can hear a package of food opening half a block away, but it doesn't hear you when you are in the same room. It growls when it is not happy. It is easily trained with a treat and a rub. If you leave a dog alone too long, he whines pitifully. When you want to play, he wants to play. When you want to be alone, he still wants to play. It's very easy to tell what a dog is thinking. A dog is thinking about food, sleep, or ..... A dog is great at begging. It gets cranky if you take away its toy or bone. You can't leave town and leave the dog in the house, because he will eat all the food in a day and tear up the house.

A dog loves to hear you say, "Good dog!" when he does what he is told to do. He wants to be petted any time. A dog left to himself will let his appearance go. His hair will become so knotted and tangled, you have to shave him. A dog leaves his toys everywhere. A dog does disgusting things with his mouth and then tries to give you a kiss.

Ladies, with this in mind, if you treat a man like a dog, he will lay his life down for you. Here are ten ways you can do this:

1. **Say, "Good dog!"** What does a dog love to hear after they do something? Good dog! They wag their tail, get excited, and might even give a bark of joy. Ultimately, this is what men want. We want our wives to be proud of us and believe that no other man could do it better.

Look for ways to encourage your husband. Once in a while, throw in an, "I'm so lucky to have an awesome provider," or "You are such an incredible dad." Ladies, you are the great communicators, so find great ways to let your husband know that he is a good dog. If he goes out of his way to do something, say "Good dog!" If he works on something, say "Good dog!" If he does something you like, say "Good dog!" If you want your dog to keep doing a trick, you need to encourage him. This is Dog Training 101!

2. **Say, "Oh, what a good dog he is" to others.** It is one thing for you to say nice things to your husband, but it is on a whole other level when you say it to someone in front of them. At a family gathering, you should say to your mom, "I am so lucky to have this guy. He is amazing!" Then follow it up with, "He's such a great dad, great provider or handyman."

You could also say, "He really takes care of me" or "He really spoils me." At that moment, your husband's spirit will be soaring. You could ask him to do anything, and he would do it! You may say, "But Scot, he isn't awesome." Remember—just say it until he becomes awesome. Speak it, then it will manifest.

Ladies, wait for your husband to walk by while you're on the phone and then say something great about him. He will light up like a Christmas tree! Put it on Facebook and Twitter! Tell the world how awesome he is. When your husband feels like he is valued for what he does, he will do more for you than you can imagine.

3. **Say, "Come puppy, come on, you can do it!"** Encourage him. I love the part in *Spiderman 2*, when Mary Jane finds out Peter Parker is Spidey. They are in an apart-

ment and have just shared a kiss. Some police sirens start going off and Spiderman looks at Mary Jane like, *Are you going to be mad if I go off and rescue some people?* But instead, she shoots him a playful smile and says, "Go get-em, tiger!" Every man in that theatre had a chill go down his spine when she said those words. We want someone to encourage us to greatness, or in a sense, push us to be great.

Ladies, don't hold your man back and then be mad because he isn't great. Behind every great man is a woman who builds her man up. She tells him he can do it. When her husband falls, she drives him to get back up and try even harder. Don't kick him when he's down; don't belittle him. It will just keep him from achieving greatness. Instead, be that person who helps him become the hero he was destined to be.

4. **Reward him, because every dog likes a treat.** Your husband had a hard day and you know it, so do something special to show him how much his hard work means to you. Now it might not mean that much to you, but the fact that you act like it does means the world to him. Men usually have wife time right when they get home. You know that today your husband worked hard, so lead your little puppy over to the couch, put his favorite drink in one hand and the remote in the other and say, "Honey, why don't you unwind a little." Honestly, this is almost as good as having sex to a man. This is a great act of love. You are showing him that you recognize how hard he worked, and you said that it meant something special to you.

If a dog brings you the newspaper, you don't hit him with it, you reward him with a treat. Likewise, if your husband takes you out for a great date, give him one hot treat!

You might say, "But I don't want him to think that he gets a treat just because he did what he was supposed to do." Think about what you are saying. Sure, I want my dog to do the trick just because I'm a good master, but the reality is, he does it for a treat. If I expected my dog to get the newspaper and I gave him nothing in return, maybe kicked him once in a while, would he continue to bring me the newspaper? Of course not! Hate to say it, but men are dogs!

Sure, a man should do things, but the reality is, if you give him one heck of a treat after a date, he will try to get you out on a date tomorrow! Wives tell their husbands they have to love them because they exist; I'm saying reward your husbands because they exist.

5. **Every dog likes a big bone once in a while.** Make sure you honor your husband with great gifts on holidays. This is the same thing I tell the men to do for their wives. Yes, men usually say they don't want any gifts, so spend it on the kids. But your kids need to see how valuable Dad is to the family. Your husband also needs to see that you value what he does. Men will get annoyed if you spend the money needed to pay bills on them— I know I do—but I love it when Holly has been putting money away slowly over a few months and then surprises me with an amazing gift. What I do is so important to her that she saved money up to bless me. Honey, you just earned yourself some pancakes!

6. **Act like you couldn't survive without him.** Yes ladies, deep down we all know you would be just fine without your husbands. Your husbands, on the other hand, couldn't survive a weekend without you! But as for men, if you act like what they do is so important and that you need them, they will feel valuable.

Ladies, your husbands need to rescue you—which is funny because men usually need rescuing most of the time! But now that you know this, act a little helpless, a little vulnerable. In the movie *The Ugly Truth,* the girl was being mentored on how to get a guy. He told her that if she had it all together, no man would want her. Wives, you need to act helpless. This drives your husbands crazy!

When Holly calls me and has a big problem, I feel like a superhero. Why? It goes along with my biggest need. Why is it when you tell your husband a problem right away, he wants to give you the solution when all you wanted was for him to listen and not try and fix you? Wives want to be valued for who they are and don't want to be fixed, but husbands want to be valued for what they do and they want to rescue you.

Remember the story about the princess who was sitting inside telling the knight about the dragon outside? The knight, without thinking, ran out of the room and came back moments later after killing the dragon. Now, the princess was mad at him because he stopped listening to her!

Come on ladies, act a little vulnerable for your husbands. If it makes them happy, why not? You will make his day by simply asking for his help in a way that makes him feel needed. How you ask is very critical though. Don't say, "Are you ever going to fix that light?" Instead say, "Honey, I'm going to fix that light. What screwdriver do I use to get the cover off?" His answer to first phrasing of the question will be "When I feel like it." However, his answer to the second phrasing of the question will be, "Stop it, you will mess it up. Let me do it." He may say it like he is annoyed, but really he feels kind of good because he is about to slay the dragon. Wives, don't be a nag; use your gifts to motivate him. A nag gets a man to do the bare minimum with a bad attitude. A Proverbs 31 woman motivates her husband with love, and there isn't anything he won't do for her.

7. **Stick up for your dog.** Dog owners can be weird when it comes to their dogs. Go over to a dog owner's house and call Fifi a mutt. Say, "What a lazy dog." That probably won't go over well. Husbands love it when their woman sticks up for them. One of the things I love about Holly is that no one gets to talk bad about me. You can talk bad about her, you can wrong her, but the second you do or say something bad to me or about me, the claws come out. I'm her man and she is very protective about me! No one better ever disrespect me. I am valuable to her.

8. **Be quick to forgive.** When your dog pees on the floor, most training has you quickly rub their nose close to it. Have you ever tried to keep a dog's nose there? Dogs gets a little crazy when you do that! Imagine holding it there for an hour, a day, a week, or even a month. Men mess up. They say things without thinking. They plan stuff without asking. They do a lot of dumb things. But ladies, when your husband does something dumb, be quick to forgive him. Don't hold his nose in it for an hour or he will fight back. Forgive and move on.

9. **Build him up before battle.** What knight wants to go out to slay the dragon after having a huge fight with his princess? Ladies, you have so much power over your husband's day. For instance, if I leave the house thinking Holly is mad at me, it really hinders what I can accomplish. But if she sends me off on my day with an encouraging word and a kiss, I will slay whatever dragon comes my way. How

successful your husband is has a lot to do with how you equip him for battle.

10. **Boy it would be cool if I had a ten, because nine does not sound as cool as ten.**

Ladies remember, if you believe in your husband, he will conquer the world, if you don't, the world will conquer him. In a sense, you choose the path for your home and family.

Why Married People Serve Pancakes Up to People Other Than Their Spouse

Just One More Swipe

I changed diapers for one third of my life (just a fact about my life). I changed diapers for fifteen years. I estimate that well over fourteen thousand diapers have been changed by these magnificent hands. They say if you do anything ten thousand times, you become great at it. Well, I became a master diaper changer. But if you would have seen me change diapers in the early days, it was a mess!

I'm guessing, but I think I have not changed a diaper now in four years, three months, seven days, and six hours, give or take a few minutes. Yet, there is something that I miss about changing diapers. It's a little personal, but I have to be honest. I truly miss the glorious cylinder of the baby wipes.

Some of you young dads know what I'm talking about. You're in the bathroom sitting down and you look over and see those God given wipes. You grab a couple of those and you're springtime fresh for the rest of the day. Those wipes have the ability to do things that toilet paper could never do.

Four years after my last experience with baby wipes, I was sitting in the bathroom and looked over and there was that cylinder of goodness. It looked as if a bright light from heaven was putting a spotlight on them. I could hear a faint sound of angels singing in the background. My heart skipped a beat. I quickly snatched the top most wipe sticking out the cylinder, then three more. When the coolness of the wipe hit the skin of my backside, I let out an "Aaaaaagh!" But at that very second, things changed. What I did not realize was that in the last four years, Clorox had come out with a bathroom cleaner that came in a baby wipe cylinder. That wipe made it feel like someone had lit my backside on fire! I could feel the flames engulf me as I let out a scream.

These Clorox wipes are representative of what having an affair is like. On the outside, it looks so good. And at first, it feels so good. But then, the fire of life's consequences hit. The lies begin eating at you. The guilt and shame begins to set in and burns inside of you. Then one day, it comes out and your whole world is on fire!

I have never seen an affair not burn down all the lives affected by it. Sure you can start over, but that is exactly where you are—at the beginning. What makes this even harder is you not only have the same marriage to conquer, but you also have all the hurt and pain of the effects of the affair added to it. The good news is that it can be done, marriages can come out stronger and better, but it takes even more work than would have been required before you had the affair. If you have had an affair, don't worry, but we do have some clean up and hard work to do in order to restore things.

Let me demonstrate how most affairs begin. I want you to see how Satan is able to get good people to do very dumb and hurtful things. Most affairs are not planned, and they happen to good people who would never dream of having an affair. In my mind, if we are aware of Satan's devices, it helps us stay clear of them. Let's say a woman is in an average marriage. She has a need to be valued for who she is. Her husband is a good man, but just doesn't treat her as valuable. She isn't first on his list, nor does he go out of his way to value her. But at work, a man in the lunchroom takes special time each day to really listen to her. He takes great interest in her life and what is going on. He pulls out her chair and carries her tray. He treats her as very special and valuable. As he meets her most important need, something in her triggers to meet his sexual need. BOOM! An affair has been birthed!

Now, let's take a look at a man in an average marriage. A man's need is to be valued for what he does. His wife lets him know constantly all the things he doesn't do right. He sees himself as a middle aged man who hasn't done anything with his life. Then here comes this young lady who thinks he hung the moon. She is in awe of him and his cool sports car. She looks up to him. She is helpless and vulnerable. She, unlike his wife, needs him. BOOM! An affair has been birthed!

In both cases, there was no just reason to have an affair. But now that we understand the most important need of a woman and a man, we can see how a good person can fall into an affair—a life destroying trap! In life, we take a lot of precautions for the 'what if's.' We have airbags for a crash. We have smoke alarms for fires. We have pool fences for the kids. So why don't we take marriage precautions? I feel like a lot of affairs could be prevented. If husbands and wives took the time to meet each other's needs. As you have seen, it doesn't take a lot—a few kind words, a date, a little time each day. If you took all the time you spent fighting and used just one tenth of that time meeting each other's needs, you would have a great marriage!

WOW and BE WOWED

Obsessed with Little People

My wife Holly is a toter. She totes everything. We have more totes than Target. Holly would move into a tote if they had one big enough to fit. We actually have cereal totes, granola bar totes, pop tart totes, pasta totes, wheat thin totes—you get the picture. My whole life is spent trying to get stuff out of the totes!

One day, one of our neighbors wanted to borrow some of Holly's scrapbook stuff. There I was playing a video game and Holly came up and said something. (Honestly, I wasn't listening.) It was something like, "Sylvia (our neighbor) is blah blah …give blah blah a tote." I, of course, said, "No problem, I got this."

An hour later, the doorbell rang and Sylvia's son said he was here to pick up the tote. I looked around and there was a tote in the middle of the floor so I said, "Here you go."

That night at eleven o'clock, as I was watching TV, Holly stomped down the stairs and blurted out, "Where are the

Little People?" I paused, because I was confused. Then I asked, "You mean our kids?"

"No! The Little People."

I continued to quip, "Are you seeing little people? Do we need to get you some special help?"

Holly was not amused by my comments and pursed her lips. Her eyes now looked like she was trying to shoot fire from them and she said, "You know what I'm talking about!"

"Honey, I can honestly say I don't, and you are frightening me just a little."

She gritted her teeth. "Where are the Little People? The Little People in the tote? The toys, Little People toys that I have been saving for nine years ever since Laken was born? The farmer guy, the business guy with the hat—"

Suddenly it clicked. "Oh those! How would I know? Honestly, I grew out of those some twenty years ago." There was a little trace of sarcasm in my voice.

Holly didn't laugh. Her eyes narrowed. "I know what happened. You didn't help Martin (Sylvia's son) get the stuff. I bet you he took them."

I said he took a tote. "I don't know if it was the Little People tote, but if so, I will get it back."

"I know you don't know, because you don't care. You don't care about the Little People. You don't care about me, about anything."

I said "Honey, I care about you. And you know what? In the morning, I'll go over there and I'll get your Little People."

"Oh, that is just like you to wait till morning to get my Little People. Just let them stay there overnight."

I stared at her for a moment. "Honey, are you thinking they might get in trouble or that they are too young to spend the night? I am very confused right now."

She shook her head and then cried out, "They have a dog! A dog! Do you know what a dog is? It's an animal that will eat our Little People and get slobber all over them."

"Okay," I said slowly. "And then I will buy us new Little People—"

"Oh, that's just like you to buy us out of it," she interrupted.

I shook my head in frustration. I have never bought us out of anything. She is acting like I'm some mob boss, buying the law off. "What do you want me to do? I will do it. Want me to go beat Martin? Kill the dog? Tell me what to do."

She began to cry. She had never really cried before, never gotten this mad before. I am so confused. Who is this woman? Her day must have had some big-time stress in it. Maybe her estrogen or some woman thing kicked in, I don't know. I'm thinking, *This is not my wife. My wife is great and she never does this stuff.* I said, "You know what honey? I refuse to fight about this, because I will not fight about things that I cannot fix. In the morning, I'll get the Little People. I'll slap the kid if I have to. I'll do whatever. I'll even sneak over there right now and break into their house if it will make you happy. I might end up in jail (which would be a better place right now) if you want. But I refuse to fight about this."

She blurted out, "You never like to fight about anything. You're just a happy man all the time. I don't have my Little People and I'm not happy, but you are."

At this point, I was so frustrated! I thought that maybe, just by chance, she missed the Little People. Maybe they were still in the house. So I got off the couch and began to walk around looking for them. I asked, "What are they in?"

"A big purple tote—a purple tote like your purple heart!" This statement made me smile, because it was so dumb. I went into the toy room and looked in the closet. I pulled some totes out, and screamed, "In a purple tote?"

"In a purple tote!"

I saw a purple tote had fallen back behind the stack. I pulled three totes out, and then got the glorious purple tote. I opened it. There, with a big light shining out of the tote, were the Little People! Hundreds of Little People smiling up at me. My heart leaped with joy, not because I got her what she so desperately wanted, but because *I was going to rub it in her face*!

As I was walking back, tote in hand, I could hear her listing all of my problems and short comings. Everything I have ever done wrong my entire life. All of a sudden, she saw the tote. A big smile filled her face, like a kid caught in a cookie jar. "Where did you find it?" Her voice was light and airy. I walked to where she was sitting. As I reached her, she asked yet again "Where was it honey?"

I then dumped the tote on her head and picked Little People up off the couch and piled them on her, asking, "Is this a Little People? Is this a Little People? What about this? Is this one of those Little People?" I grabbed the farmer and acted like he was talking to her. "Hey, look at me! I don't care about anything! I buy my way out of everything!" Then we laughed for a long, long time.

You would be hard pressed to find a woman who doesn't want to be beautiful and have her husband stand in awe of her. God put a need inside of every woman to want to be beautiful for their man. From the time a woman was a little girl, being beautiful was on her mind. When my daughter Savannah was three years old, she would glide into the room, smile and say, "Am I pretty Daddy?" At three years old, she desired to be beautiful. Do you know how many times my boys asked me—or even cared—if they were lookin' good? Not too often. If they are looking good, it is only to impress a girl who is beautiful.

> *"The king is enthralled by your beauty."*
>
> Psalm 45:11

I love that word "enthralled," because it completely de-scribes what your wife wants to be in your life. She wants to walk into the room and have you be enthralled with her beauty—to be literally speechless. Once again, God has made man's needs compliment woman's needs. Men, we want to be enthralled. Beauty captivates us. A woman wants to be enthralling, and men desire to be enthralled.

Men, do you remember the first time you saw her? OMG! Your heart raced, your tongue was dry. You couldn't believe that someone so beautiful would give you the time of day. She needs you to be that captivated with her today. *But Scot, she's not enthralling.* If you act enthralled long enough, you will become enthralled. But a woman also wants you to be equally wowed by what is inside her. My mom is 67 years old and when she enters the room, my dad still has to take a pause to breathe in her beauty. Forty-five years of marriage, and my mom still takes his breath away!

As you become interested in your wife's beauty, she will too. As you begin to treat her like she is the beautiful gift God gave you, she will instinctively begin to become this. As we learned earlier, love your wife as Christ loved the church, then she will become all you desire. When she feels beautiful, she will become beautiful.

In counseling, the root cause of a lot of fights is that women think their husbands don't notice them anymore. Showing that you do notice her beauty is an important part of acknowledging who she is.

Here are some tips for men to help make their wives feel beautiful:

- Let's start with the basics. Obviously, grab any chance you can to tell her how beautiful she is. Don't wait for her to ask, "How do I look?" Walk into the room and say, "You look unbelievable. I truly am a lucky man." And you can do the same thing on a "sweat pants day" at home. Say something like, "How are you so beautiful even when you don't try?" That's a good one (and I should get a nickel every time someone uses it)!

- Whenever your wife walks into the room, stop what you are doing. When you do this, you will be meeting both her need to be the most important thing in your life, and her need to be captivating. Just look at her until she asks, "What?" Then simply say, "You are so beautiful." Then she will spout out something like, "You are weird." But her heart will have skipped a beat. Twenty years ago, this was a lot harder and annoying to do because if you were in the middle of watching a game on television, you had to stop to say she was beautiful. Meanwhile, you might have missed the go-ahead touchdown. Today, thankfully we have TiVo, God's gift to men.

I believe this piece of technology has saved many marriages, because men can just pause what they are watching on television and pay attention to their beautiful wives.

- When you are at church or a party, let your wife catch you staring at her from across the room. Then shoot her one of those, "Man, I'm lucky" smiles.

- Take an interest in what your wife is wearing. She will probably want you to look at five different pairs of shoes, trying to figure out which one goes best with her outfit. She will also come out with two different tops and hold them up, wanting you to tell her which one looks the best on her. Let's be honest, to men, they all look the same. Yet I have learned to stop what I'm doing and pretend to really care. I act like I'm really having a tough decision. I might say something like, "Honey, hold up the other one. Hmmm. Let me see the first one again. Yeah, that one brings out your eyes." Then off she goes with a smile on her face, only to return a few moments later with a different shoe on each foot. So I say, "Turn sideways, now turn the other way. Wow, they both look good! Walk a little, let me see. You know, I personally like the one on the right. (Of course, I just choose one randomly.) This means the world to Holly.

    Try to remember a piece of jewelry your wife wore with an outfit. Then a few weeks later, say, "Remember that little dolphin necklace you wore with that teal outfit you wore to church a few weeks ago?

I think that will go great with this outfit." This will melt your wife's heart and she will probably take her clothes off and make some pancakes right there!

This goes for wives too. Ladies, suppose you decided to watch football with your husband because it was important to him. In the beginning, all the players may look the same to you. You don't know the difference between running backs, fullbacks, offensive guards or wide receivers. But in time, you'll learn who is who on the playing field, and now you can better interact with your husband about football.

- When your wife is talking, nothing else matters—no cell phones, no texting, no kids, no television-glancing. When she talks, it is like you are talking to Jesus. Remember, she wants to be beautiful to you—inside and out. Her inner beauty is probably more important to her. You need to look her in the eyes, breathless at the beauty who is talking to you. Engage in the conversation and don't let your mind wander. Show her how beautiful she is by simply focusing on her.

To sum it all up, go back to your wife's most important need. She wants to be number one in your life. If she is in the room, be captivated. If she is talking, be captivated. Gasp for air when she comes around. Men, an amazing thing will happen when you do this: That driving passion you had while you were dating will return.

Here are some tips for ladies:

- Be captivating! If you are going out, put some time into it. If you look better when you go out with your friends than with your husband, you need to change. Make sure you look good for him. Now this can mean sweats and a tee, but pay attention to the whole package. A man likes to see beauty. That's his need. Fulfill his need.

  Here is a tip for marriages beyond five years and a few kids. When you first got married, your wife came to bed nearly nude. She gradually started wearing a shirt, and then added sweat pants. Now, she is fully dressed coming to bed. Come on ladies, be alluring—a little sexy. You might think, *Well, then he will want sex.* I have news for you: He always wants sex! You could come to bed in plate armor, and he will want sex. *But what if the kids come in?* They shouldn't do that. The marriage bedroom is your haven. Lock the door so they have to knock. *Scot, they won't feel secure.* That makes no sense. Children get their security from their parents having a great relationship. (I wasn't ever allowed in my parent's room, and I grew up pretty secure.) Your kids can knock. They will be just fine.

- Flirt! It is a gift God gave you. I can't flirt. When I try to flirt, Holly thinks I look ridiculous. But she can flirt! She will sit on my lap. She will give me a little kiss on the neck. Yes, ladies, you want your man to pay attention, but he is a dog. If you want a dog to pay attention, you have to give him a reason.

Be sexy at times. Be captivating and enthralling. When you walk into a room, own it!

- Ladies, make your outer appearance important to you. A lot of ladies work hard at looking good, but then when they get married, they let themselves go. How you look is very important to your husband, and it needs to be important to you. *Well, this is just how I am.* Okay, but we don't let guys have that excuse. If you deal with a weight issue, realize it's unhealthy and can lead to a lot of diseases. Get medical help if you have to, but fix the problem. I'm not being mean—just honest. Yes, it is a lot of work, but the rewards are priceless. You'll feel better, and you'll feel better about yourself. Stop making excuses to live below the level that God intended you to live. You can do all things through Christ!

CHAPTER
12

IHOP is Open 24 Hours

The Starbucks Fight

My wife loves her coffee and she loves Starbucks nearly as much as she loves me. (I say that hopefully.) She is the Norm of *Cheers* at Starbucks. Everyone is like, "Hi Holly," "Hey Holly," "How you doing Holly?" and "Did you have a good birthday Holly?" It is crazy!

Savvy's first words were, "Iced grande vanilla latte with two shots." I, on the other hand, hate coffee, always have and always will. And you coffee people are always trying to get me to like coffee. "Oh, you have to try it my way; couple sugars, some cream." You know, you could put a couple sugars and cream on dirt, but it would still taste like dirt. I hate coffee but I love my wife, so I find myself daily at Starbucks.

When I first started getting Holly coffee, it took me a while to learn the language. I felt like a tourist trying to order a simple cup of coffee in France. "I would like a small iced coffee."

They would respond, "You mean tall."

"What? No, I want a small, not a tall."

"Our tall is a small." (I feel like I'm in a Dr. Seuss book: "Your tall is a small. Well, that's not nice at all," said the Hoo Haa on a ball.)

"Your small is a tall?"

"Yes."

On another note, I think the whole drink world is annoying. You order a small soda at Burger King and they say, "We don't have a small." That makes no sense. Your smallest drink would naturally be a small.

I won't give in on this point (which annoys my wife). "I want your smallest drink."

"You mean our medium?"

"I want your small, which would be your smallest drink." (Except at movie theatres, where you order a small and they deliver a three liter jug and say, "That will be $17.")

So, I'm on the phone with my mom and pull up to a Starbucks drive thru on a Saturday morning. I was a little surprised that there was only one car in line. I thought, *God is good to me!* I had to make a sharp turn to pull up to the rear quarter panel of the car to get in line. On my left was parking and an aisle for cars to get through. All of a sudden, *Bam! Bam! Bam!* I turn my head and look and a big bald-headed rhino of a guy is banging on my window. He's huge! I roll my window down an inch and he says, "Get your blankety-blank out here or I'm gonna kick your blankety-blank."

I'm like, "What?" I was really confused. I couldn't figure out why he wanted to beat me up?

"You blankety-blank, if you want to cut in line, you have to deal with me."

I look over and there was a long line of cars going through the parking lot. Apparently, the front car had left an aisle open for cars to go through, which I'd mistaken for the end of the line. I'd made an honest mistake, but this idiot made me mad. "Get out of here. It's not the sixth grade and I'm not going to fight you after gym. Go back to your car!"

"You get in the back of the line," he ordered, waving his fat finger towards the back of the line.

"Whatever!" I shooed him away. He stomped back to his car at the back of the line. I noticed his wife in the passenger seat, her head down in shame. I whipped my car around, my face getting redder by the second. I got right behind his car. I'm on his bumper. I'm basically in his back seat right now. I start to talk to myself. "Come pound on my car, I'll pound your head. Think you're all bad? You haven't had 5'4" of me all over you. I'll send you straight to see Jesus, then resurrect you, and send you back again!"

He went back to his car and adjusted his rearview mirror and just sat there staring at me. I just shot him a stare right back.

All of a sudden, I heard God say, "Buy their drinks."

I said, "No way!" I was so mad!

God said, "Buy their drinks."

I said, "NO."

He said, "Love your enemies."

I said, "Your Word says You cut down my enemies like the noon day grass. Cut him down. You cut him down and I'll buy his wife a drink and make his little bald head go 'boop.'"

Again, I heard Him say, "Buy their drinks."

I took a deep breath and through gritted teeth said, "Fine, I'll buy their drinks." So when I got up to the little order window and I ordered my drink, I said, "And I would like to buy the drinks for the car ahead of me."

She responded, "Are you sure?"

I replied, "Yeah, I'm sure."

"Well, you should have heard what he said about you."

Really? Baldy told Starbucks on me? Like I'm gonna be grounded or something? I said, "Yeah, I'll buy his drinks anyway." So I pulled ahead and then watched as he pulled up to the pay window. I saw him go to give the lady money, but she shook her head and pointed back to me. He tried again and she shook her head yet again.

At this point, one of the most magical things of my life happened. The man's wife's head snapped toward him, and she started talking in an animated fashion. You could tell she was letting him have it. He was being cut down like the noon day grass. Then, his car door slowly opened and he began to walk back towards me, his head hung like a six year-old in trouble. When he got up to my window, I rolled the window all the way down and said, "Can I help you?"

"Well, I'm sorry. I apologize for the way I was back there." And then he looked over to his wife and you could tell she was looking at him like a little boy and motioning for him to go on. He said, "And thank you for buying me the drinks." He walked back to his car and got in and drove off. I got the fullness of joy and screamed out, "Love does work, all the time!"

You are probably thinking, *What does this story have to do with anything?* Well, we are going to talk about loving someone when maybe you don't feel like it, and doing something for someone simply because it is the right thing to do.

I'm going to say something so profound, so revolution-ary that ladies, you will never guess what it is. Here goes: *Men need lots and lots of sex.* I know that is a cutting-edge revelation. The only way I could have gotten that informa-tion was from the Creator himself. It's funny to me that women know this, yet it isn't as important to them as it should be:

> *Let the husband render to his wife the affection due her (this means holding hands, being romantic, talking and sharing), and likewise also the wife to her husband. The wife does not have authority over her own body, but the husband does: DO NOT DEPRIVE ONE ANOTHER EXCEPT WITH CONSENT for a time, that you may give yourselves to fasting and prayer, and come together again so that Satan does not tempt you because of your lack of self-control.*
>
> I Corinthians 7:3, NKJV

I want to start with that last part of this verse: Come together so Satan does not tempt you. Ladies, here is an example that will help you understand the need for sex. Sex to men is like food is to the human body. You like to eat every day, correct? What happens if you go a few days without food? You get a little cranky, a little irritable.

I remember when I wrestled in high school. During my senior year, I cut 25 pounds in one week. To do this, I did not eat for seven days. Understand this, I hate green beans. I hate the smell, the texture, and especially the taste of green beans! However, on day six of my fast, Momma was cooking dinner and had an open can of green beans right in front of me. I went over and smelled those green beans. It was a glorious smell. I had done well at not eating, but at this point I could not control myself. I grabbed a small handful of green beans out of the can and shoved them in my mouth. Oh my, they were so good!

Let's compare this to sex. Let's say that your husband has not had sex in a few weeks. At the office is this "green bean woman." She is nasty and in no way compares to you. An affair is never okay, but he is so tempted; he'll have any *green beans*. If he is well fed, nasty green beans wouldn't tempt him the least bit.

Ladies, I tell the men that the Bible says they need to love you as Christ loved the church. They need to love you because you exist. They don't get to make up reasons not to love you and to lay down their lives for you. Take it a step further: I don't want them to love you half-way, going through the motions, without commitment to excellence. On that same note however, the Bible says your body is not yours, therefore, saying "no" to sex is not an option. Why shouldn't you be held to the same standard? Ladies, you should be rocking his world!

Scot, he doesn't pay attention to me. You start rocking his world, and he sure will pay attention to you. He is like a dog. If you give him a treat and feed him well, there is nothing that dog won't do for you. But, if you don't feed your dog and he smells some food over the fence, that dog will do all he can to get that food.

Sex is so very important to your husbands, so it needs to become important to you. You need to get crazy with it once in a while. When he comes home, hide in a closet, pop out and jump him. Seriously! Give him stories to tell his buddies. Remember how I said you will talk about your husband? His behavior determines what you say. Likewise, your husband is going to talk about your sex life, too. And you determine what he will say.

We had a dog named Sammy. Peyton's only chore was to feed Sammy. Sammy was a great dog. He never got into the trash. One day, I went outside and Sammy had been jumping up the trash can, tore a hole in a bag and was eating the trash. I went and grabbed Sammy to rub his nose in it and give him a little swat. Walking to the trash, I noticed the bowl with Sammy's food was empty. I went in and asked Peyton how long Sammy had been without food. Peyton said, "I don't know, but it has been a long time." Well of course, I didn't discipline Sammy because it really wasn't his fault. He was really, really hungry.

Ladies, understand this, if your husband doesn't get fed by you on a daily basis, he will still eat. That is a fact! He will probably jump up into a trash can to get some scraps. Your husband will deny it and you will say things like, "Not my husband." But, you are wrong. It doesn't mean that he is having an affair, but at bare minimum, he's found a substitute like checking out some porn. I'm not saying porn is okay, but ladies, if the dog isn't getting fed, can you really be that mad at him for eating scraps out of the trash?

I have seen wives leave their husbands over porn. So I ask, "When was the last time you made love to him?"

"A few months ago."

Really? And you're mad at him?

My Bible says to feed him when he wants to be fed. You are not following the Bible (or common sense) if you are not properly doing this. You want to be all holier than thou about his sin, but your sin is really, really mean!

Here is a great example that ties back to my Starbucks story. Holly loves coffee. She needs a cup of coffee every day. Of course, she can go a day without it, but it annoys her. Nearly every day, I go and get her coffee from Starbucks. Honestly, I don't love getting the coffee for her. (I don't hate it, but I don't enjoy it nearly as much as she does when she gets the coffee!) Let's say that the Bible says it is a sin for her to get her own coffee. But it also says that it is a sin for me to withhold the coffee from her. Would it be right for me to get her coffee once a week, maybe a few times a month? Suppose then that I find out she is brewing coffee on her own? Do I now get to be the moral police? How mean is that?

Knowing how much Holly loves coffee and how much I know she needs it, I would do my best to make sure she gets coffee every day. Plus, I would become a barista—I would aspire to make her the best cup of coffee possible. I would try and surprise her with coffee. Maybe I would wake her up in the morning with a hot cup of coffee. I probably would show up at her work and find a closet to give her a cup. Maybe I would give her coffee on a drive or in a theatre. I would give her coffee stories that none of her girlfriends would ever believe!

Scot, we have kids and we are so busy. I don't feel in the mood. When he says he is too tired to talk to you or take you out or lay down his life for you—is that suddenly okay? You can't have it both ways. If he has to lay down his life for you, you need to give it up for him. You expect him to give up cable television for a date, but maybe you need to give up Facebook. Freud actually said that everything a man does one way or another is to get sex. It's important to your husband, so it should be important to you.

Here's a tip from Holly:

Here is a trick. Remember, women are incubators. If you will preheat the oven in a sense, throughout his whole day he will be thinking about it—the romance, the touch, the feel. By the time he gets home, you will be hot and ready. Just make it what you do. You may not want to do the dishes, but it is what you do. What we tell the men is do it, and do it with a happy heart. Sometimes it is awesome; sometimes it is what we do and it is awesome just because you are loving your husband.

It is important to make him always feel like you are in the mood and it is not a chore. If he talks to you but acts like it is a chore, is that any fun? If he is doing something special for you but you can tell he doesn't want to do it, is that fun? You are thinking, *Fine, just don't do it.* The same thing goes for sex. Yes, at times it might be a chore, but make sure he never knows that because his sexual ego is so fragile. It is like a piece of fine china. You have to be so very careful with it. Make him feel like he is so desirable that he fulfils your every need.

Let's talk candid. This is what a hooker does. It's a job she has to do. But she knows if she acts super into it, into him, he will come back and pay top dollar for her. Part of rocking his world is engaging in it. You want your husband to be engaged with you while you are talking. Well, the same thing goes for sex. Don't let your mind wander, be in the moment with him. Make it all about him! If you feed him well, you will be surprised how many arguments are avoided when your man is full!

YOU'RE IN, NOW GET OUT

The Torturer and the Pincushion

When should you prepare? Before or after the event? Obviously before. Yet, how many marriages fail because they are not prepared? How many fights go on forever because you have two people who are not prepared? Preparation is the key to winning any great endeavor. Preparation is a key part of getting in and out of fights.

My brother has a missionary heart. Every year he goes to Africa. Good for him. I don't share that same desire. If I go on a mission trip, it is to Jamaica. They also need Jesus. Well, for five years, Jason has been trying to get me to go to Africa with him. I always jokingly say that God would have to come down in a burning bush and speak to me about going and even then, I would only consider it.

One morning last May, I woke up and told my wife, "I don't know how it happened, but I think I am going to Africa with Jason." After years of refusing to go to Africa, I finally agreed to go with him. I don't know if Jason drugged me or what, so I called my dad because he had gone there the previous year, and said, "Dad, how did that happen?"

My Dad said, "I don't know. I woke up one morning and your tricky little brother had duped me into going to Africa last year." He paused. "Now here is the problem with your brother. I love him very much, but he will not give you all of the information up front. He will feed you the information slowly, and eventually you will get all of the information when it is too late."

Two weeks before we were scheduled to leave for Gulu, Africa, Jason said, "Hey Scot, we need to go get a few shots." Now the key word in this is *few*. Let's break this down together. What is a few? Obviously it's more than one shot. Two would be a couple. Three might be a few, right? Four would be a stretch, but might still be considered a few. Five would be stupid. So I'm like, it can't be five. But even four seems like a lot of shots.

Jason also mentioned that it would be "a little bit of a trip to Africa." That is what he said. *A little bit of a trip*. So my mind did the math. I was thinking what constituted a little bit of a trip, you know, fly over-seas, drive time, lay overs. I was thinking maybe sixteen, seventeen, eighteen hours. That seemed like quite a little bit of a trip.

So we pulled up to Evvax (in the Greek that means, *house of great pain*). As we were walking in, I held the door for my brother, and as he walked by, he said, "Oh, by the way, it is a thirty-eight hour trip to Gulu." Thirty-eight hours? What, are we paddling a canoe there? How long am I on the back of a burro on this trip, Jason? Thirty-eight hours? Before I could get my hands on Jason, he was already in the door and in the company of potential witnesses.

It was my turn to walk into Evvax. One word describes this place: *Dungeon*. Brick walls painted white, floors dingy. There was a coldness in that atmosphere that were like lingering pain. I noticed all the walls were bare except one. On one wall, there was a massive map of the world. Along the side of the map was a list of all these crazy diseases I thought we cured thousands of years ago. As I walked up to the map, I noticed that these diseases had colors next to them. Then I noticed that the map had matching colors on it in order to show where these diseases currently are. I began to see a recurring pattern. Every colored disease was in Gulu, Africa. That is, every disease except the Japanese flu. I thought *Just give them that one—then they can brag they have them all.* My mind instantly reverted back to shots as I recalled that Jason said we'd be getting a few shots.

We sat down with the lady, whom we will refer to as "the torturer." She wanted to go over all of the diseases to see which ones I wanted to get shots for. She named the first one and it had the word 'plague' in it. I think any disease with the word 'plague' in it has to be taken care of, so I quickly said, "Yes please!" Then she proceeded to name three more, each having words like "death," "infestation," "plague" in them. I also said "yes" to each one of these. After the fourth one, I became curious and inquired, "Hey, are these combined into a couple of shots?"

The torturer smiled an evil grin. "No, no, each is a separate shot."

Well, this was a game-changer for me. We were already at a 'few' shots. So now when she read off a disease, I would say, "Well, now how deadly is that one? What are my chances? Give me some statistics? What happens if I do get that disease?" For every single one, she would say these horrible things like, "What will happen in the first 24 hours is that your kidneys will shut down. Your heart will begin to start bleeding, and the blood will slowly ooze from all your orifices." It seemed like every disease ended with, "And you will DIE!" So needless to say, I responded with, "Yes, please, I would like two of those shots if possible."

Finally, when we got through the list, she had twelve shots for Scot. Yes, you read that correctly—twelve shots! She said to me, "Would you also like to have a flu shot?" That hit me hard. Were they running a special—buy twelve and get the thirteenth free? So I replied, "Sure, give me your stupid flu shot." On a side note, the guy working the front desk said I would have the record for the most shots. That's a super-cool record to have. I should add that I got the stupid flu shot, even though I don't ever get the flu.

The torturer left the room to get her tools of pain. I sat in silence, unwilling to even recognize that my brother existed. I was thinking of great ways to get back at him. I want you to picture how she came back into that room. (I know she did this for show, and to be funny.) She had four shots in each hand and she was twirling them in between her fingers. She looked like Edward Scissor Hands.

I was sitting on the little torture table with my shirt off, and she smiled and said, "I want you to look straight ahead." (She seemed to enjoy her job a little too much). In my mind, I thought she was just doing one shot at a time, but she wasn't. She was doing four or five at a time! So when that first wave hit me, I sucked in a huge breath, shook a little, and let out a, "Whoa! That hurt!" Then she hit me with the second batch. The pain was so intense! I had thoughts of grabbing the shots and jamming them into her and my brother. I clenched my teeth while my whole body shook. Sweat seemed to be pouring out of me. I let out a small screech of pain, and the torturer said, "Hold on." I thought, *Hold on? Hold on why?* Then she jammed five more shots into my arm. It felt like she was squeezing pure Clorox bleach into my veins! My arm felt like it was on fire. Each millisecond, when you thought the pain could be no more horrific, it seemed to double. I let out a scream so loud they said they heard it in the parking lot. It hurt so badly! I said, "Jason, I am not ever getting another shot in my life. I want you to know that. I will not get any more."

She finally said, "You're done." Then, as we walked out of that place, my mind began to process what I had just experienced. The serum for every disease known to man (except for the Japanese flu) was flowing through my body. I began to feel invincible. I felt like nothing could hurt me. As we walked out, I saw some gum on the ground and thought, *I could pick that up right now and eat it. It wouldn't touch me. It wouldn't hurt me at all because I am immune to everything.*

See what preparation does? Had I not gotten the shots before I went over to Gulu, I would have been afraid, very timid. I would have been careful not to touch anyone or anything. But because I got all those shots, I was prepared. I went over there confident. I wasn't scared to touch any-thing, hug anyone, or shake anyone's hand.

The same thing goes for our marriages. In fights, we don't know what to do. We aren't prepared for how to get out of the fights. Once you are prepared, you will have more confidence. You won't be afraid, walking on tip toes throughout the day. You will be able to react and act out of confidence instead of fear.

Meeting each other's needs should eliminate a lot of fights. But now let's spend some time on getting out of fights. Have you ever jumped into a pool that was a lot colder than you expected? Your natural response was to get out as fast as possible. This should also be your natural reaction to fights. The next chapters are crucial, because like it or not, arguments will happen. The Bible says, *iron sharpens iron*, and you can't have that without a few sparks. Holly and I have sharpened each other over the years. Our goal is to get you out of fights with your spouse in five minutes or less. These next chapters hold the keys to accomplish this.

Remember, all fights are birthed out of fear. We get rid of fear by injecting love into the situation. Please remind yourself of that. As a rule of thumb, injecting love should be your first action to get out of a fight, because love conquers all.

Here is one of the biggest relationship killers and limiters. Nearly all marriages have this cancer in them. If it is not removed on a daily basis, this cancer will spread. I'm talking about un-forgiveness. When I say we must forgive, I'm not talking about the world's forgiveness, where we say we forgive but we still want our enemies hit by a bus. I'm talking about God's forgiveness. The Bible says to forgive as Christ forgave. Jesus was whipped until the skin hung off His back. Huge thorns were pushed into His head. He was nailed to the cross and had a spear shoved into His side. Yet, on the cross, what did He say? Did He say, "Father forgive them, but make sure they pay for their actions. I forgive them, but avenge me." No! He said, "Forgive them, they know not what they do." In other words, I don't want them to have the consequences for their sin. I want only good for them.

Forgiveness is a complete letting go. It means forgetting the past completely and not wanting a loved one to have consequences for their actions. I know that's not fair, but unforgiveness only hurts you. You forgive, not for them, but for *you*. So let it go!

When my kids were toddlers, I would give them a sippy-cup full of milk. Problem is, they never brought it back. We would find that cup a week or a month later. We found one cup over five years later. When we opened the lid, pure evil came out. What a rancid smell! That is what un-forgiveness does inside of you. It spoils you. I know that's not fair, but life isn't fair. Is it fair to hold onto that unforgiveness and hurt all your other relationships? Is it fair to lose out on the future God has for you because of your past? Is it fair for the person who wronged you to steal even one more day out of your life, with you holding onto a grudge?

Suppose I was driving down the freeway and someone cut me off. I mean, really did me wrong. Would it make sense for me to pull over and not move until they came back to apologize? Should I sit there until they get what's coming to them? I'm going nowhere, while they are off ahead, probably unaware that I'm still fuming. You have to let anger and hurt go. I'm talking about all unforgiveness, because it will spoil you. It will hinder you and your marriage and all other relationships. How do you get rid of unforgiveness? Love! Inject some love into it. Love always drives out fear.

The secret is to pray for those who hurt you. Every night, pray that God blesses them and gives them a great day. At first, that's a very hard prayer. But over time, it gets easier and easier. Then one day, you pray it and you actually mean it! It is at that point that you know you have forgiven. The "spoiled milk" that has been in there for a while takes some time to get rid of, but if you get in a habit of letting go, forgiveness will clean out your sippy-cup.

It is very important that after an argument, you forgive as Christ forgave. You don't want to slide in another dig, hurt him/her with your pouting, or get even in some way. Forgive. Let it go and never think about it again. The fight is in the past. Every time a non-forgiving thought comes, hit it with some love. Say, "God bless them! I love them! What nice thing can I do for them?" Hit it with love. To have a great marriage, you have to become a great forgiver. Forgiveness has to be something you do as fast as you can when you get mad and upset. It takes work at first but in time, it becomes a habit that is as natural and as easy as breathing.

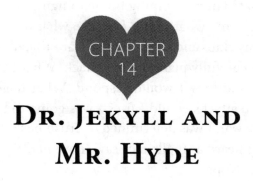

CHAPTER
14

DR. JEKYLL AND MR. HYDE

In the Rough

Once while playing golf, I was on the eighteenth green. It had been a long hard battle. The course had nearly broken me. My score was already in the 90's (in case you don't know, that is not good). I'd just doffed another drive into the sand. I was annoyed and unhappy. My cell phone rang. It was Holly, so I answered, forcing a happy, "Hi Hon!"

"YOU SAID YOU WOULD BE HOME AT 4. IT IS NOW 4:10. WHILE YOU'RE OFF GOLFING AND HAV-ING A GREAT TIME, SOME OF US HAVE THINGS TO DO!" Yes, it was 4:10. Yes, I said I would be home at 4, but the way she attacked, it made me attack right back.

"Oh calm down. You're late all the time." Who would have guessed that was the wrong thing to say? She then started going off on all my faults so I just hung up on her.

Then, I continued the fight, talking out loud to myself. "Tell me to be on time? You're never on time. I'm a man. If I want to golf, I'll golf. I'll golf all day if I want. I work all week. Guess what? I'm not coming home tonight, I'll be golfing. No one tells me what to do. *I* tell me what to do!" Then I grabbed my clubs and hurried to the car, still talking to myself. I was carefully planning my attack. What I'd say, what she'll say, and how I would respond. What huge, hurtful bomb-type attacks would I use? I was going to be victorious in this war. I was determined to crush her!

Then I heard a small voice say, "Love her."

I said, "Nope!"

"Love her! Do what you have been teaching."

Yes, I had been talking about the power of love, but that was for others. "That stuff doesn't work in my situation."

"Love her!"

This went on for a few minutes until I finally conceded, *Fine! I will love her.* I took a deep breath, focused on some good thoughts and instantly something in me changed. It was as if a cloud had lifted and I could really see what was going on. Before, I had no faults, but now I could see where I went wrong. I was late, that is a fact. I told her I would be home at 4. She does do a lot of stuff and is an amazing wife and mother. She was counting on me. Man, that was truly rude of me. Now, my battle plan had totally changed. I was wondering how to tell her I was sorry, so I crafted an amazing attack of love. I was surely going to be victorious!

I opened the door to the bedroom and there she stood in the doorway of the bathroom. She was so mad! She actually looked like she was on fire. I quickly said, "Honey, I am so sorry. Sorry about being late, sorry about my response. It was so rude of me. You do so much and I, the idiot, do this."

"Oh, don't give me that!" she said. (I knew this was coming, and I was *prepared*.) I walked toward her as she let out a string of verbal reminders of just how much of an idiot I was. I grabbed her tight and continued on with the apology. She made a half-hearted attempt to get out of my hug, but you could tell her heart wanted the embrace. She let out another small attack, but I saw it coming and easily dodged her words. I came back with some more love. Then finally I felt the anger break free. "Well, you are dumb sometimes," she said playfully.

We then started a small kiss that seemed to go on and on. Fast forward thirty minutes, (Holly said it was more like four minutes). I am now in bed, looking up at the ceiling and in an audible voice, I said "God, if this is what it feels like to be wrong, I don't ever want to be right!"

How many fights do we hold on to? How many times do we allow anger and negative emotions to control us? If we just injected some love, it is amazing how our minds would clear up so we could see how to navigate out of the fight. Sometimes it seems that we work so hard to stay in the fight! What if we worked that hard to get out of the fight? Why hold onto anger and resentment? The quicker we let it go, the quicker we can get on to a great marriage.

Scot, I can't just let it go. It's too hard. It's a lie. Holly and I were in a battle. I mean, we were dropping bombs left and right—a classic fight. Holly was as mad as I have ever seen her. She was right in the middle of letting me know what a jerk I was, when suddenly, the phone rang. She stopped mid-sentence and answered the phone with the sweetest,

"Hello" I have ever heard. "I'm great, how are you?" The conversation went on for a few minutes as I stood there as perplexed as I would have been if she had sprouted wings and started flying around the room. "Alright, talk to you later. Have a great day. Bye." Then she hung up the phone, and Dr. Jekyll was gone and Mrs. Hyde picked up right where she left off.

"Wait! Hold on! You cannot be mad if you just want to! I just saw you happy as can be. You have the ability not to be mad. I saw it with my own two eyes. It was like seeing Big Foot and Mother Theresa in the same body!"

What is the fuel that starts a fight and then keeps it going? Emotions! If you get a husband and wife in control of their emotions, how long do fights last? Not long at all. Funny thing is, we have the power to control these emotions, as we saw with Holly. You have probably been in a fight when a family member or friend walked in, and you turned on a big ol' smile. You have the ability to do this. Once again, you just have to inject some love into the situation.

I used to teach these principles mainly to women, because I assumed women were the more emotional creatures. But things have changed. I have a lot of husbands who pout for days and are mad for weeks. So this is for whoever can't control these emotions.

Why in the world would you want to stay mad? Why would you want to keep that nasty stuff in your cup? Dump it out. Does being mad do any good? Have you ever gotten over being mad and said, "I'm so glad I was mad. Man, that really made things a lot better"? You can get a lot more accomplished in the relationship when you are cool and collected. When you are in control, you are the rudder in the relationship.

Thoughts produce emotions. If you think sad thoughts, you will feel sad. If you think happy thoughts, you will feel happy. By controlling your thoughts, you can control your emotions. If you think about what a jerk your spouse is, you will feel angry. If you force yourself to think about how awesome your spouse is, you will stop being mad.

The Bible says to cast down all arguments and thoughts that are contrary to God's Word and make them line up with the Word. "All" actually means "all." Get rid of all of those angry and negative thoughts. In my 21-day book, I talk about the law of substitution. This law says you can have millions of thoughts, but only one at a time. If you have a thought that is not producing right emotions, you simply need to substitute the right thought. You can't think angry and happy thoughts at the same time. Inject some love. Put some good thoughts in and get out of the emotions that do you no good. I like how that scripture says to *cast down the thought.* This means to be aggressive with your thoughts. Get those thoughts in control.

My dad is from the backwoods of Wisconsin. He grew up riding horses so he knows horses. We heard stories of him riding the ol' sledding horse at four years old, down the snow-filled roads as grandpa drove beside him. My dad knows his horses. But as for me, I'm a city boy. I only know what I see in Westerns. They make it look so simple. Giddy up, whooo, there you go, you are an expert horse rider. When I was twelve, my dad took us horseback riding. This old cowboy came from the barn dragging this thing that looked like it was a horse at one time. As it got closer, it didn't get prettier. It had a patch over one eye and looked like it was losing hair with splotches of skin showing.

The old cowboy said to me, "Here you go son. Ol' Gus is his name." He helped me up onto Ol' Gus and then walked away. I sat nervously for a moment and then hesitantly said, "Giddy up." The horse did nothing. "Giddy up!" I said, a little more forcefully as I gently kicked my heels into the horse's side, quite scared I would give the ancient beast a heart attack. The horse whipped its head around and slowly walked over to an old tree pretty far from the group. Along the way, I kept trying to turn the horse or at least stop it. But the horse was going to do what the horse wanted to do. The horse began to eat from a small patch of grass, and then with sickening noise, relieved himself of yesterday's meal.

My dad called for me to come over, so I pulled the reins and said, "Come on boy." The horse yanked its head back down and continued to eat. My dad motioned again, so I shrugged my shoulders and cried out, "The horse won't come!"

My dad trotted his steed over to me. "What in the world are you doing?"

"Stupid horse won't go. The old thing is broke."

My dad smiled, and said, "You have to take control of that horse."

I shook my head. "I tried, but he won't go."

"No son, grab them reins and yank them as hard as you can. You have to show that horse who is boss! If you don't control the horse, the horse will control you." I took a deep breath and grabbed the reins tightly. "Come on, yank those things!" I yanked those reins to the right and gave the horse a huge kick. The horse shook and tried to yank its head back down. "Again!" my dad said, so I pulled even harder. Then the horse turned and took off. It tried to go left.

I yanked it back right. It went too far right. I yanked left. That horse got going too fast, so I yanked back. This battle went on for a few minutes until it finally only took a little tug left or right to get him to obey.

You have to treat your emotions the same way. For many, these emotions have been allowed to do whatever they want for a long time. They're sitting over there in the corner, controlling your life. It's time to take control. At first, your emotions will fight you. You have to yank those thoughts into place. You have to declare: I WILL THINK GOOD THOUGHTS ABOUT MY SPOUSE! Yank those thoughts. Be aggressive with them. If they start to veer off the trail, yank them back on track. The Bible says to think only on those things that are good, holy and praise-worthy. Meditate on these things. The world "only" actually means "only." It's your job to take control of any thought that is contrary to this. If you do this for a few days, all of a sudden just like the horse, it will become easy. Just a little tug here and a little tug there, and you will be able to control your emotions. Then it will become something you don't even think about anymore. It will become a habit.

But for a time, you'll have to yank your emotions in place. You have to be in control of them. If you don't control your emotions, your emotions will control you. They will drive a wedge in your relationship. You might think, *But she won't listen unless I escalate.* She doesn't listen *because* you escalate. You may get her to do what you want, but she will do it begrudgingly and resent you. Who wants that? I want my wife to do things because she loves me. How do I get that result? With anger and hurt, or with love? With love.

For example, Holly would get so upset at my socks on the floor. She'd get really mad. Sure, I picked them up during a little fight. I would be thinking about all the stuff I do, and that she is mad about stupid socks. One day, she just stopped getting mad. A few weeks later, I saw her picking up my socks by the bed and I was puzzled. "Sorry, babe," I said.

She said, "No big deal. I decided not to let it bug me. One day, if you figure out it means a lot to me, you might start doing it on your own." That hit me hard, so I started making an effort to pick up those stupid socks. I don't do it all the time, but I do it a lot of the time. Best thing is, we don't fight about it anymore.

Two things happened. She decided not to let something small upset her. She was in control of her emotions. She could waste twenty minutes fighting over it, or love me and take seven seconds to put them away. Is it fair to her? No, I'm a slob. But it *is* love. Marriage is about picking your battles, finding out what's worth fighting for, and deciding what's really no big deal. It's about accepting one another's good qualities *and* those annoying qualities.

When someone screams at you or attacks you, what is your natural reaction? Of course, you become defensive and fight back. But if someone comes to you in love and asks you to do something, you are a lot more open to change.

If something bugs you, should you attack? Nothing good ever comes out of that. Instead, put some love into the circumstance. Maybe it is something like socks all over the floor that keeps getting you upset. Take a moment and ask yourself if it's worth the fight. Honestly, is it really that big of a deal? I leave my socks out. I admit I'm a slob. But I do have a lot of good characteristics. Holly decided to love me in my weakness. *Instead of seeing my socks as me not loving her, she sees them as her loving me.* If your wife doesn't cook dinner as often as you want, come home and cook dinner yourself or go out and buy dinner. She is busy with the kids and the house and all the other stuff. Instead of seeing it as her not loving you, praise God that you have been given an opportunity to love her.

If your husband says something dumb (as men do), instead of being upset about him being insensitive, embrace the opportunity to love and forgive him for being stupid. This can literally change your entire marriage.

What if you loved your husband into what you wanted him to do, rather than trying to fight him to become what you want? For instance, let's say that he is texting while you are talking to him. Instead of getting mad because he is not loving you, look at it as an opportunity to love him. The Bible says that a kind word turns away wrath. I wonder how many fights could be avoided if we simply became aware of our tone and our attitude. The way in which we respond to each other is probably responsible for over 75 percent of our fights. How we say something or ask something reveals our attitude.

If your spouse says something rude, in a nice voice say, "Stop, you don't mean that." Most of the time that will snap them out of it. If you snap back, what happens? The Bible says don't return wrath for wrath, but respond with love. If Holly is grumpy, being kind snaps her out of it. But when I mirror her mood, we get into a huge battle.

Holly is the best at this. When I'm grumpy, she comes over, kisses me on the cheek and says, "Knock it off, you big baby." I wish I could snap her out of a mood that quickly. Inject love into the moment. Really work on your tone, inflection, attitude, and response. Honestly, this will keep you out of most fights. What's better than getting out of a fight in five minutes? Not getting into a fight.

Spend some time writing down what you got out of this book in a notebook of your own. Then, write out the changes you will be making. I think it would be important to go over this list on a daily basis for 21 days (the amount of time it takes to form a new habit). Then review your notes on a monthly basis thereafter. Change comes by hearing and hearing.

Don't get discouraged if you mess up. It's called life. You should get excited that you have the opportunity to be better tomorrow. Marriage is a lot of work, but like anything you work hard for, a life with the person God gave you that's full of joy and passion is surely worth the effort. Work hard at getting out of those fights in five minutes. In the beginning, it might take thirty minutes, then twenty minutes, eventually ten minutes, and ultimately five minutes. (It's like working out; you can't bench 250 pounds right away.) When you hit that five minute mark, celebrate—make a big deal out of it. As human creatures, we strive toward things that give us pleasure and run away from things that cause us pain. If getting out of a fight in five minutes gives us pleasure, then subconsciously we will start to make that happen on a regular basis.

No one said marriage would be easy, but those who work hard and learn to get along will tell you that marriage is made up of the best things life has to offer. They say that *Happily Ever After* is for real, and it can be this way for you and your spouse, if you make it so!

PRAYER OF SALVATION

God loves you—no matter who you are, no matter what your past. God loves you so much that He gave His one and only begotten Son for you. The Bible tells us that "...whoever believes in Him shall not perish but have eternal life" (John 3:16 NIV). Jesus laid down His life and rose again so that we could spend eternity with Him in heaven and experience His absolute best on earth. If you would like to receive Jesus into your life, say the following prayer out loud and mean it from your heart.

Heavenly Father, I come to You admitting that I am a sinner. Right now, I choose to turn away from sin, and I ask You to cleanse me of all unrighteousness. I believe that Your Son, Jesus, died on the cross to take away my sins. I also believe that He rose again from the dead so that I might be forgiven of my sins and made righteous through faith in Him. I call upon the name of Jesus Christ to be the Savior and Lord of my life. Jesus, I choose to follow You and ask that You fill me with the power of the Holy Spirit. I declare that right now I am a child of God. I am free from sin and full of the right-eousness of God. I am saved in Jesus' name. Amen.

If you prayed this prayer to receive Jesus Christ as your Savior for the first time, please contact us on the Web at **www.harrisonhouse.com** to receive a free book.

Or you may write to us at
Harrison House • P.O. Box 35035 • Tulsa, Oklahoma 74153

The Harrison House Vision

Proclaiming the truth and the power

Of the Gospel of Jesus Christ

With excellence;

Challenging Christians to

Live victoriously,

Grow spiritually,

Know God intimately.